Karolinum Press

MODERN CZECH CLASSICS

Jiří Weil
Lamentation for 77, 297 Victims

Translation from the Czech by David Lightfoot
Afterword by Jindřich Toman

KAROLINUM PRESS 2021

KAROLINUM PRESS
Karolinum Press is a publishing department
of Charles University
Ovocný trh 5/560, 116 36 Prague 1
Czech Republic
www.karolinum.cz

Cover and graphic design by Zdeněk Ziegler
Set and printed in the Czech Republic by Karolinum Press
First English edition

Cataloging-in Publication Data is available from the National Library
of the Czech Republic

ISBN 978-80-246-4533-9 (pbk)
ISBN 978-80-246-4534-6 (pdf)
ISBN 978-80-246-4536-0 (epub)
ISBN 978-80-246-4535-3 (mobi)

ABOUT THE AUTHOR

Jiří Weil (1900–1959) was a Jewish Czech writer, translator, and essayist.

Born into an upper-middle class family in the small Central Bohemian village of Praskolesy, Jiří Weil moved to Prague to study Slavic philology and comparative literature at Charles University; in 1928 he earned his doctorate. A committed leftist at the time, he translated for the press department of the Soviet trade representation in Prague when he was still a student.

In 1933 the Czechoslovak Communist Party sent Weil to Moscow to work as a translator for the Comintern. His harrowing experiences in the Soviet Union inspired him to write *From Moscow to the Border* (1937) upon his return; fiercely critical of Stalinism, the novel resulted in his expulsion from the Communist Party.

Having narrowly escaped Stalin's purges, Weil's life was again in jeopardy when Nazi Germany invaded Czechoslovakia the following year. During the occupation, Weil was assigned to work in Prague's Jewish Museum, where confiscated Jewish property was processed. To avoid being transported to the concentration camps, Weil faked his own suicide.

After the war, Weil would return to Prague's Jewish Museum to work as its senior librarian. Although Weil had mentioned Judaism only once in his writings before World War II, it now became the focus of his writing. His most famous novel, 1949's *Life with a Star*, was criticized both by the ruling Communists and by members of the Jewish community. This novel, as well as Weil's anti-Stalinist stances, led him to be expelled out of the Czechoslovak Writers' Union in 1951. *Life with a Star* is now considered a classic, championed by writers like Philip Roth.

Weil's oeuvre is notable for its range of styles, from the documentary fiction of *Memories of Julius Fučík* to the experimental prose poem *Lamentation for 77, 297 Victims*. A common thread in his work, however, is a brave stance against the horrors of totalitarianism.

Smoke from nearby factories shrouds a countryside as flat as a table, a countryside stretching off to infinity. It is covered by the ashes of millions of dead. Scattered throughout are fine pieces of bone that ovens were not able to burn. When the wind comes, ashes rise up to the sky the fragments of bone remain on the earth. And rain falls on the ashes, and rain turns them to good fertile soil, as befits the ashes of martyrs. And who can find the ashes of those from my native land; there were 77, 297 of them? I gather some ashes with my hand, for only a hand can touch them, and I pour them into a linen sack, just as those who once left for a foreign country would gather their native soil so as never to forget, to return to it always.

Paper boxes sit on a shelf of soft wood painted brown. In the boxes names are arranged in alphabetical order. There are 77,297. These are the names of victims from Bohemia and Moravia. Each name has a transport number, year of birth, last place of residence, and date and place of death. Sometimes the date and place of death are not given. No one knows when and where they died. The names are inscribed on the walls of the Pinkas Synagogue, which stands next to the Old Cemetery. Thus will their memory be preserved.

MOREOVER ALL THESE CURSES SHALL COME
UPON THEE, AND SHALL PURSUE THEE,
AND OVERTAKE THEE, TILL THOU BE DESTROYED
-- Moses 28:45

That day snow fell, though spring had already come, snow that immediately melted and turned into mud, that day people stood helpless, raising their fists in the air or crying, that day wheels cut into wet earth, and the rattle of military trucks drowned out the shouts of despair.

Josef Friedman, forty-four, immigrant from Vienna, jumped from the fourth floor of his apartment building. He died slowly in the street. The ambulance couldn't get to him because the military had closed off the street. When the ambulance finally reached him, Friedman was already dead. That was 15 March at 2 o'clock in the afternoon.

SO I RETURNED, AND CONSIDERED ALL THE OPPRESSIONS THAT ARE DONE UNDER THE SUN: AND BEHOLD THE TEARS OF SUCH AS WERE OPPRESSED, AND THEY HAD NO COMFORTER; AND ON THE SIDE OF THEIR OPPRESSORS THERE WAS POWER, BUT THEY HAD NO COMFORTER.
-- Ecclesiastes (Keholet) 4:1

Death entered the city that day, accompanied by fifers, bearers of horsetails, death's-heads and the rattle of drums. People tried to flee from her, but Death's legs were faster, she caught them in their flight, in trains and at the gates of border-crossings.

People were standing in a long line outside the police headquarters on Perštýn. They had been there since the early hours, they had arrived when it was still dark. At 9 o'clock the gate opened. An SS-man in black uniform stepped out. He said: Jews—out of the line. He said it in German, as he stood on the sidewalk with his legs splayed wide, and a Czech guard translated.

THEREFORE WILL I CAST YOU OUT OF THIS LAND
INTO A LAND THAT YE KNOW NOT, NEITHER
YE NOR YOUR FATHERS; AND THERE SHALL YE
SERVE OTHER GODS DAY AND NIGHT
-- Jeremiah 16:13

LENA 21.VIII 1934 – 16.X 1941. JAN 12.IX 1937 – 16.X 1941. VALERIE 31.X 1893 – 3.XI 1941. VALERIE 6.I 1908 – 11.III 1944. EVA 19.IX 1939 – 16.X 1944. VĚRA 14.X 1932 – 20.VIII 1942. ZOFIE 5.VI 1889 – 22.VIII 1942. BONN HANUŠ 21.VIII 1942. TEREZIE 6.I 1894 – 22.X 1942.
VI 1873 – 22.XI 1942. RUDOLF 20.X 1867 – 6.VIII 1942. MARIE 25.XI 1879 – 1.IX 1942. VILÉM 21.XII 1907 – 6.IX 1943. MARIE 11.V 1869 – 8.VIII 1942. BORAL ISIDOR 18.III 1872 – 28.X 1942. CHARLOTA 18.II 1902 – 28.X 1942. B
KA 19.VIII 1879 – 22.X 1942. OTA 16.XI 1911 – 6.IX 1943. GERDA 11.V 1909 – 26.X 1942. SIMON 16.X 1881 – 28.VII 1942. GISELA 2.IV
JOSEFINA 11.VII 1914 – 6.IX 1943. BEDŘICH 11.II 1916 – 1.V 1944. JOSUA 1.X 1896 – 27.IV 1942. IDA 30.XI 1881 – 27.IV 1942. IR
VIII 1942. VIKTOR 1909 – 1.XI 1941. EVELYNA 21.IV 1887 – 20.IV 1943. RICHARD 11.VII 1911 – 20.I 1943. FRANTIŠKA 2.II 1883 – 2
MARIE 3.XI 1886 – 19.IV 1942. BORGES JIŘÍ 6.V 1884 – 28.VII 1942. VILÉM 11.V 1887 – 28.IV 1942. IRMA 28.II 1890 – 28.X
BORGZINNER ERICH 27.IX 1903 – 28.IV 1942. CHARLOTA 17.V 1902 – 26.X 1942. EDITA 3.XI 1927 – 26.X 1942. BORKOV
NA 19.VIII 1937 – 18.XII 1943. BERNÁT 3.VIII 1940 – 18.XII 1943. MARIE 2.III 1905 – 18.XII 1943. BORKOVEC JAN 29.IX 1899 – 2
BORKOVSKÝ JOVÁ MARIE 12.IX 1903 – 25.I 1943. BORLOVÁ AUGUSTA 7.II 1861 – 22.X 1942. BORN HERBERT 9.V 1904 – 6
LFGANG 24.VIII 1936 – 6.IX 1943. GRÉTA 10.VI 1908 – 3.XI 1941. BORNHEIMOVÁ GERDA 26.II 1906 – 6.X 1942. BORN
1942. BOROŠ EMIL JENŐ 19.V 1911 – 11.III 1942. ARNOŠTKA 8.III 1876 – 22.X 1942. IRENA 15.I 1907 – 20.VIII 1942. BOROV
VI 1942. BORSKÁ HANA 10.X 1913 – 21.X 1942. JÁLENA 8.III 1876 – 22.X 1942. LILY 14.IX 1911 – 19.X 1942. MARIE 6.IX 1
VSKI MARCEL 24.VII 1921 – 30.IV 1942. BOŘKOVCOVÁ LUDVÍKA 16.III 1882 – 20.VIII 1942. BOSCHAN JINDŘI
31.VIII 1878 – 5.VIII 1942. VILMA 14.XII 1894 – 6.IX 1943. HEDVIKA 9.XI 1881 – 20.VIII 1942. IRMA 30.VI 1885 – 6.IX 1943. F
IAOVÁ EMA 19.VIII 1875 – 19.X 1942. BOUCHALOVÁ MARIE 2.II 1909 – 31.X 1942. BOŽÍNOVÁ OTÝLIE
LILY 14.IX 1909 – 15.I 1942. BRABENCOVÁ MARIE 9.III 1877 – 15.X 1943. BRADA JIŘÍ 15.IV 1868 – 15.X 1942. ANNA 26.X
1942. MARTA 12.V 1907 – 6.IX 1943. HELENA 16.V 1941 – 6.X 1941. TOMÁŠ 26.I 1943 – 6.X 1943. IRMA 5.IV 1878 – 28.VII 1942. JANK
1925 – 15.I 1942. RŮŽENA 10.III 1885 – 28.VII 1942. BRADLEOVÁ ZDENKA 6.I 1910 – 20.I 1943. BRACHOVÁ MARIE 28.II 189
VI 1942. BRAMER JINDŘICH 1.III 1880 – 30.IV 1942. JULIE 21.II 1888 – 30.IV 1942. BRAMMER KURT 4.IX 1912 – 25.IV 194
IX 1942. ISIDOR 25.VII 1895 – 28.IX 1944. TEREZIE 7.III 1902 – 19.X 1944. EVA 4.X 1925 – 9.X 1944. LEA 11.I 1929 – 19.X 1944. J
NA 4.VI 1894 – 20.VIII 1942. OSKAR 8.III 1890 – 9.I 1942. BERTA 12.IV 1858 – 22.X 1942. CHARLOTA 22.IV 1886 – 31.X 1941
ANDELS ARNOLD 17.II 1872 – 16.I 1944. BEDŘICH 28.VIII 1896 – 27.IV 1942. JOSEFA 28.II 1903 – 21.IV 1942. EDVIN 6.II 1882 – 23.
943 OTA 22.V 1908 – 23.I 1943. EGON 30.VIII 1897 – 1.IX 1942. FRIEDA 5.IV 1906 – 1.IX 1942. EMIL 29.X 1873 – 31.X 1941 KARL I
V 1879 – 31.X 1941. AMÁLIE 13.XII 1887 – 31.X 1941. LEOPOLDA 1.VIII 1914 – 31.X 1941. KAREL 5.VII 1879 – 15.I 1942. FRANTIŠ
98 – 28.X 1942. HANA 9.II 1907 – 28.X 1944. TOMÁŠ 1.X 1933 – 28.X 1944. ANITA 2.X 1936 – 28.X 1944. OSKAR 28.VIII 1876 – 28.X
TA 22.XII 1894 – 20.VIII 1942. RICHARD 19.XI 1865 – 19.X 1942. OTÝLIE 4.I 1875 – 31.III 1943. VALTR 2.I 1892 – 23.III 1943. ZIKMU
0.IV 1878 – 22.X 1942. ADÉLA 17.II 1874 – 15.X 1942. EMA 30.VI 1881 – 28.VII 1942. IRENA 15.X 1878 – 15.VIII 1942. BEDŘIŠKA
VIII 1873 – 22.X 1942. MALVÍNA 23.VII 1877 – 24.VIII 1942. MARTA 5.X 1894 – 28.X 1942. OLGA 21.IX 1880 – 28.III 1944. HAN
EISKÝ KAREL 2.V 1888 – 20.VIII 1942. MARKÉTA 29.VIII 1886 – 28.VIII 1942. GERTRUDA 5.VII 1919 – 20.VIII 1942. HERMÍNA
GUSTAV 8.VIII 1871 – 22.X 1942. ANITA 30.VIII 1932 – 20.VIII 1942. OTÝLIE 27.VIII 1870 – 22.X 1942. RUTH 28.II 1920 – 10
VIII 1942. ELA 20.I 1905 – 20.VIII 1942. BRATOVÁ REBECA 11.VI 1880 – 15.X 1942. BRÁTTOVÁ PAVLA 31.IX 1910 – 15.I 1942. BRAUCH EDGAR 23.XI 1919
KAROLÍNA 6.XII 1885 – 23.I 1943. BRAUCHBAR RICHARD 1.I 1902 – 15.X 1944. BRAUN ALFRED 6.III 1875 – 15.XII 1943.
VI 1883 – 22.X 1942. MARKÉTA 5.VII 1893 – 11.X 1942. CECILIE 14.IV 1922 – 30.IV 1944. ALOIS 31.I 1858 – 10.X 1942. ANDOR 14
11.VI 1906 – 20.VIII 1942. ANNA 28.IV 1912 – 20.VIII 1942. VĚRA 8.VI 1938 – 20.VIII 1942. ARTUR 27.VIII 1892 – 28.IX 1944. GRÉTA 31.III
GERHARD 30.VII 1935 – 6.IX 1943. DAVID 12.VII 1894 – 26.X 1944. MARIE 15.V 1896 – 26.X 1942. EDUARD 18.X 1896 – 25.IV
FRANTIŠEK 21.X 1903 – 22.X 1942. GEJZA 22.X 1886 – 28.IX 1944. GUSTAV 19.II 1872 – 25.IV 1942. KAREL 18.V 1877 – 25.IV 19
43. HUGO 4.II 1897 – 23.X 1944. HUGO 16.X 1906 – 6.IX 1943. HILDA 16.III 1914 – 6.IX 1943. ISIDOR 21.VII 1900 – 30.IV 1942. HE
TUR 10.XI 1929 – 30.IV 1942. TOMÁŠ 18.III 1936 – 30.IV 1942. JOSEF 2.VI 1865 – 15.XII 1943. BERTA 13.XI 1871 – 15.XII 1943.
TA 1.XII 1897 – 6.IX 1943. KAREL 30.XI 1903 – 28.X 1942. KAREL 10.XI 1910 – 9.I 1942. LEO 14.X 1886 – 31.III 1943. LEO 29.VIII 18
1942. LEO 9.IX 1913 – 20.I 1943. ANNA 15.IV 1881 – 20.I 1943. LEOPOLD 11.VII 1884 – 30.IV 1942. LEOPOLD 26.VII 1915 – 18
42. FRANTIŠEK 24.V 1888 – 28.VII 1942. VALERIE 18.I 1896 – 28.VII 1942. HANA 7.XI 1921 – 28.IV 1942. OSKAR LEOPOLD 15.
30 – 15.III 1944. VALTR 21.I 1898 – 15.XII 1943. VIKTOR 7.XII 1887 – 12.X 1944. JULIE 6.II 1886 – 12.X 1944. ANNA 31.VIII 1900
V 1944. BOŽENA 3.XI 1921 – 30.IV 1942. ELIŠKA 3.VII 1890 – 21.X 1944. GERTRUDA 25.II 1917 – 18.XII 1943. HEDVIKA 9.II 1871
1944. IDA 5.XII 1885 – 6.IX 1943. HANUŠ 11.IV 1909 – 6.IX 1943. RICHARD 1.V 1912 – 6.IX 1943. ILSA 30.VII 1915 – 22.IX 1942. IRMA
1913 – 6.IX 1943. MARTA 8.VII 1921 – 21.IV 1942. MARTA 9.III 1923 – 4.X 1944. JANA 27.XI 1941 – 4.X 1944. MATYLDA 28.X 1876 – 22
A 6.XII 1880 – 28.VIII 1942. RŮŽENA 26.XII 1872 – 22.X 1942. SERENA 16.V 1917 – 18.XII 1943. MARIANA 13.III 1939 – 18.XII
ZANA 29.V 1910 – 1.X 1944. BRAUNBERG GUSTAV ROBERT 17.I 1896 – 29.IX 1944. BRAUNER ERICH 19.III 1898 – 3.X
RICH 17.X 1920 – 3.X 1941. KURT ? – ? SIMON 21.XI 1881 – 31.III 1942. LEO 8.VIII 1899 – 6.IX 1943. IDA 27.VIII 1899 – 1.IX 1942
ELD FRANTIŠEK 16.VII 1893 – 6.VII 1942. BREDA ERICH 16.VII 1897 – 28.IV 1942. RŮŽENA 26.XII 1900 – 4.X 1944. HANUŠ 20.IX 1904 – 8.IX 194
1.I 1925 – 15.I 1942. BRECHER OSKAR 10.VII 1886 – 25.VIII 1942. ROBERT 22.XII 1890 – 6.IX 1943. GERTRUDA 25.VI 1902 – 6.IX 194
REITENFELD ARNOŠT 19.VII 1887 – 20.VIII 1942. ANNA 24.IV 1904 – 20.VIII 1942. RUDOLF 22.IV 1911 – 1.X 1942. HEDVIKA 16.XI 190
IX 1943. MARTA 22.XI 1898 – 20.VIII 1942. BREITLER KAREL 5.XI 1895 – 6.IX 1943. MARIE 18.XI 1897 – 6.IX 1943. LEO 8.IX 1922 – 6
11 1942. BREJ.NÍKOVÁ OTÝLIE 3.V 1901 – 15.X 1942. BRENDER KAREL 26.III 1888 – 19.X 1942. AMÁLIE 6.XI 1896 – 19.X 1942. J
RTUR 24.VII 1882 – 20.VIII 1942. BEDŘICH 25.VI 1902 – 6.IX 1943. ELIŠKA 21.V 1910 – 6.IX 1943. KAREL VIKTOR 17.IX 1932 – 6.IX 1943. ERICH
366 – 21.III 1943. OSKAR 15.IX 1888 – 1.X 1942. OSKAR 7.VII 1891 – 24.X 1944. OSKAR 25.X 1897 – 28.IX 1944. MARTA 29.III 1894.
RUDA 8.XI 1899 – 15.X 1942. FRANTIŠKA 15.IX 1872 – 26.X 1942. HERMÍNA 2.I 1886 – 6.IX 1943. MARTA 6.X 1909 – 18.V 1942. STI
R LUDVÍK 17.XI 1879 – 28.IV 1942. JANA 12.V 1889 – 28.IV 1942. OTA 31.VII 1893 – 26.X 1942. RICHARD 5.II 1881 – 28.VII 1942. AL
JAN 28.VIII 1903 – 9.I 1942. JULIUS 14.III 1889 – 16.X 1941. FRANTIŠKA 17.IV 1895 – 16.X 1941. KLÁRA 16.II 1859 – 19.X 1942. BRET
1945 ANNA 24.XI 1911 – 6.X 1944. JANA 13.XII 1935 – 6.IX 1944. MICHAL 23.I 1941 – 6.X 1944. GUSTAV 31.VIII 1876 – 22.X 1942. JOSI
V 1906 – 31.V 1944. MILADA 21.III 1906 – 31.V 1944. TOMÁŠ JIŘÍ 7.III 1933 – 1.IX 1943. JULIUS 20.II 1904 – 9.I 1942. KAREL 24.V 1901
MAX 28.VIII 1877 – 31.X 1941. JULIE 30.V 1876 – 7.IX 1942. HERMÍNA 12.II 1878 – 31.X 1941. KAREL 24.V 1901
NII 29.IX 1926 – 15.I 1942. ZDENĚK 12.V 1928 – 15.I 1942. BRETTSCHNEIDEROVÁ ELSA 30.II 1885 – 15.I 1942. LILY 28.IV 191
15.III 1944. ERVIN 19.III 1894 – 4.X 1944. KAREL 8.XI 1905 – 1.X 1944. BETY 15.XI 1882 – 20.I 1943. BRIESS ALFRED 15.VII
1879 – 25.VIII 1942. BLANKA 11.VII 1887 – 21.X 1941. BRICHTA ARTUR 1.I 1888 – 15.IV 1944. MARTA 28.IX 1897 – 15.IV 1944. FRA
6.XI 1925 – 6.IX 1943. ANNA 25.II 1930 – 15.VIII 1944. HERMAN 6.V 1897 – 29.IX 1944. ANTONIE 22.VII 1892 – 12.X 1944. JURAJ 2.X
V 1908 – 20.VIII 1942. BRÍK VILÉM 21.XII 1896 – 6.IX 1944. BRILL ARNOŠT 1.VII 1898 – 26.X 1942. BEDŘICH 8.XII 1885 – 1.IV 1942. EMA
1879 – 22.X 1942. FRANTIŠEK 14.III 1890 – 11.III 1942. OSKAR 1.V 1896 – 15.X 1942. ZDENĚK 4.XII 1903 – 21.X 1942. ANNA 22.II 1909 – 21.X
1941 HELENA 16.III 1934 – 21.X 1941. BEDŘICHA 20.II 1908 – 26.X 1942. BERTA 19.II 1883 – 19.X 1942. IRENA 21.VII 1892 – 28.X 1942. JIN
ENA 27.II 1870 – 15.IX 1943. TEREZIE 29.I 1887 – 6.IX 1943. VALERIE 12.VII 1902 – 26.X 1943. ZDENKA 9.IV 1905 – 14.VII 1942. ZOFI
V 1942. BRINGOVÁ ANNA 9.II 1901 – 14.VII 1942. BROCK ALFONS 26.II 1888 – 3.XI 1941. BEDŘICH 7.IV 1895 – 3.XI 1942. RŮŽEN
92 – 15.XII 1943. JINDŘICH 31.XII 1909 – 28.X 1944. JIŘÍ 21.VII 1901 – 20.I 1943. LUDVÍK 21.XI 1900 – 28.X 1942. EMILIE 15.X 190
1943. KAMILA 20.II 1872 – 22.X 1942. RŮŽENA 30.III 1865 – 22.X 1942. BROD ALBERT 15.VII 1904 – 22.X 1942. ALFRED 11.II 1887
I FRANTIŠEK 9.V 1913 – 21.X 1942. ANNA 16.IV 1900 – 15.X 1942. DAVID 8.III 1873 – 30.III 1942. EMIL 14.V 1875 – 15.X 1942. SEMI 1887.
ALICE 31.VII 1931 – 31.X 1941. KAREL 2.III 1893 – 29.IX 1944. OLGA 21.IX 1890 – 6.IX 1943. JAN 10.III 1932 – 6.X 1944. LUDVÍK 14.
1885 – 4.VIII 1942. OTA 6.VII 1888 – 28.X 1944. TEREZA 12.VII 1895 – 28.X 1944. MARIANA 20.IV 1926 – 28.X 1944. RICHARD 17.X
2 – 16.X 1941. RUDOLF 1.VIII 1868 – 9.VII 1942. OLGA 26.VI 1875 – 15.XII 1943. ALICE 27.XI 1910 – 20.VIII 1944. ALŽBĚTA 18.V 1903 – 20
VÍNA 28.III 1885 – 15.VIII 1942. MARKÉTA 24.II 1889 – 25.VIII 1942. HEDVIKA 17.XII 1890 – 25.VIII 1942. JETY 16.III 1880 – 31.X 1941
EK 7.X 1908 – 19.II 1945. MARIANA 12.XI 1897 – 20.VIII 1942. VILÉM 9.IV 1909 – 19.X 1942. ZDENĚK 4.XII 1943 – 9.IX 1944. MARTA
1886 – 3.XI 1941. JANA 5.III 1919 – 3.XI 1941. MATYLDA 2.II 1868 – 10.VIII 1942. META 31.III 1911 – 3.XI 1941. OLGA 29.I 1890 – 15.XII
BERNA 16.V 1889 – 12.X 1944. ZOFIE 12.III 1887 – 28.IX 1944. BRODAVKA EMERICH 3.IV 1895 – 28.IV 1942. ELSA 12.IX 1896 – 28.I
UDOLF 16.XI 1899 – 28.IV 1942. HILDA 21.III 1909 – 28.IV 1942. KITY 5.V 1937 – 28.IV 1942. TEREZIE 3.VIII 1891 – 16.X 1941. BRODA
RIC 6.XII 1872 – 16.X 1941. MINA 21.IX 1896 – 16.X 1943. BRUNO 13.VII 1929 – 16.X 1943. OSKAR 25.IV 1922 – 26.X 1942. BRODHEIM
BRODSKÝ...

They issued laws meant to bind, hound, wear-down, pulverize, crush and destroy the spirit—spiteful and senseless laws. And because they only thought about how to enrich themselves— for they loved things and were willing to steal, to murder and to plunder,— they first issued laws that made it possible for them to seize property.

Rudolf Jakerle of Kobylisy had saved money his
whole life so he would have something to live on
in his old age. He kept it in the bank. On 28 March
he wanted to withdraw a certain amount, but they
told him at the bank that they could not release any
money without proof of Aryan status. Rudolf Jakerle
went home agitated. An hour later he suffered
a stroke and died.

IN WHOSE HANDS IS MISCHIEF,
AND THEIR RIGHT HAND IS FULL OF BRIBES.
-- Psalms 26:10

Then they passed countless other devious laws, of which no one could keep track: they forbade the use of streets, some only during business hours, and others on Sundays and holidays, some that were paved with cobbles, some that were asphalted, and some that were actually highways. One forbidden street was Ermine, and no one knew where that could possibly be. They also forbade certain foods, fruits, onions, garlic and spinach. They forbade parks, woods, waterfronts, libraries and galleries. Some of these laws were passed in secret, including an order that Jews not leave their homes after 8 pm.

On December 15, 1939 an SS commando stormed the Aschermann café on Dlouhá Street, the Ascherman was a café Jews were allowed to patronize, mostly emigrants and people who had no place to live and nothing to live on went there. It was exactly 20:05. The SS pulled leather gloves on their hands and began beating Jews. Chairs fell and tables were overturned, thickening blood dripped onto the broken cups as they lay strewn on the floor. The patrons were dragged out of the café, packed into wagons and were taken to a villa in Střešovice that housed the anti-Jewish unit. There in a courtyard next to the garage they were again beaten long and hard, then interrogated. Some were let go, others were led away. Those who were led away disappeared forever.

FOR DOGS HAVE COMPASSED ME: THE ASSEMBLY
OF THE WICKED HAVE INCLOSED ME:
THEY PIERCED MY HANDS AND MY FEET
-- Psalms 22:17

ANNA 1.IX 1854 · 20.IX 1942 ANNA 16.I 1883 · 4.VIII 1942 ANNA 22.I 1886 · 4.VIII 1942 ANNA 15.1890 · 12.III 1942 AUGUSTA 25.IX 1876 · 27.VIII 1942 BERTA 4.
HERMÍNA 19.XI 1863 · 19.X 1942 HERMÍNA 13.I 1880 EVŽEN 1.VIII 1907 · 3.XI 1942 IRMA 2.XII 1879 · 25.X 1942 JANA 3.I.VIII 1883 · 9.X 1942 KURT 25.VI 19
OLGA 1.VI 1906 · 12.X 1942 OTYLIE 14.IV 1901 · 22.IX 1942 PAVLA 15.V 1908 · 8.IX 1942 REGINA 12.I 1879 · 16.X 1942 RŮŽENA 16.V 1864 · 16.IX 1942 ZOFIE 10.XI
1888 · 9.V 1942 ALFRÉD 8.VI 1887 RŮŽENA 13.X 1883 RENATA 21.I 1915 · 14.VII 1942 VILÉM 16.IV 1877 · 6.IX 1942 PAVEL 21.V 1887 EMA 4.XII 1894 · 6.IX 1942 PAVEL 12.I 1901 · 6.IX 1942 VILÉM 18.I
OSVALD 21.XI 1907 · 21.IX 1942 VILÉM 16.IX 1893 VILÉM 16.IV 1877 · 6.IX 1942 PAVEL 29.V 1887 EMA 4.XII 1894 · 6.IX 1942 PAVEL 12.I 1901 · 6.IX 1942 VILÉM 18.I FERDINAND
MATYLDA 15.II 1903 CERTRUDA 7.II 1979 · 15.I 1942 RŮŽENA 13.VI 1885 · 30.VII 1942 MAYERHOFFEROVÁ LUDMILA 3.IV 1903 · 31.X 1942 MAZLIAC
SCHIMA ZIKMUND 10.V 1889 CHANA 23.IX 1897 · 15.I 1942 MEHREROVÁ ELIŠKA 24.XII 1860 · 16.V 1942 MECHNEROVÁ FRA
LAURA 16.VIII 1893 · 4.X 1942 FRANTIŠEK 9.II 1900 MARIE 22.V 1909 ADRIANA 23.XI 1933 · 2.X 1942 FRANTIŠEK 7.VIII 1900 · 18.IV 1942

MIRKO 18.III 1919-28.IX 1944 * OTA 29.X 1904-28.II 1944 * OTOMAR 8.X 1878-15.II 1942 * RICHARD 30.X 1876-15.X 1942 * ROBERT 25.XII 1877-28.IV 1942 * VIKTOR
EFA 18.XI 1890-1.IV 1942 * JULIE 11.XI 1884-23.IV 1942 * KAMILA 16.III 1900 MILOŠ 23.IX 1907 ZDENĚK 23.XI 1930-23.X 1942 * KITY 11.X 1891-6.IX 1943 * MATYL
1942 * GUSTAV 3.VIII 1886 MARKÉTA 10.III 1891 GERTRUDA 3.II 1914-15.VII 1942 * HANUŠ 22.VII 1915-6.IX 1943 * HYNEK 18.V 1881-15.X 1942 * IGNÁT 26.VI 1903
1878-24.XI 1942 * JAQUES 18.VIII 1885-18.V 1942 * MARCEL ERVÍN 28.VIII 1906-28.IV 1942 * MAREK 8.VII 1902-28.IV 1942 * MILADA 23.IX 1895-12.
ZZ III 1942 * PAVEL 26.XII 1902-19.XII 1942 * FRANTIŠKA 5.IX 1862-22.X 1942 * MEISTER Alexander 30.X 1883-11.IV 1942 * MEISEL
MARKÉTA 16.IV 1880-16.X 1944 * MEISTER EMIL 9.III 1883-29.VIII 1942 * STĚPÁNKA 26.V 1889-26.X 1942 * MEISTERLES ARN
A 22.II 1901-18.IV 1942 * VIKTOR 13.II 1885-22.X 1944 * LUDMILA 4.III 1868-7.IX 1942 * RŮŽENKA 18.X 1889 OSKAR 10.VIII 1905 VILÉM 8.XI 1908 KURT
E 10.XI 1899-28.X 1942 * VILÉM 21.X 1913-29.X 1944 * MALVÍNA 13.III 1913-4.IX 1942 * ZDENKA 13.XII 1939-1.IX 1942 * Milan 7.IV 1943-8.V 1944 * ANNA 30.X 1868-15.X
MARTA 27.III 1894-6.IX 1943 * HELENA 27.VI 1887-15.II 1942 * REGINA 10.III 1868-26.X 1942 * MELZER Augustin 12.VIII
ZOFIE 26.XII 1888-15.X 1942 * MENGELE FRANTIŠEK 8.III 1871-16.V 1942 * MENDEL
1942 * EDUARD 17.XI 1855-10.XII 1942 * RŮŽENA 20.V 1862-8.IX 1942 * JOSEF 23.XI 1859-15.III 1942 Natalie 20.XII 1868-1.IV 1942 * KAREL 21.X 1885 MARIA 19.
30.XII 1942 * ZOFIE 25.IX 1886-15.X 1942 * MENINGEROVÁ Barbara * MENSEL Arnošt 29.II 1889-21.X 1944 * MENZEL FI
1942 * VALERIE 30.V 1893 LI.IV 1942 * MENZELES EMIL 28.IV 1879 ERNA 20.X 1891-28.IV 1942 * MERGER Ervín? 1906-? * MERKSAME
11.V 1942 * MERORY ALFRED 22.II 1885 NELA 19.IV 1891 ALŽBĚTA 21.X 1915 HANUŠ 18.XI 1912-28.IV 1942 * MERTEN FELIX 11.IX
ROŽENA 20.III 1867-19.X 1942 * MESSINGER HANUŠ 8.X 1899-26.IV 3 * KAMILA 28.VII 1893-15.II 1942 * MESSNER EMANUEL 5.
XII 1873-15.X 1942 * JIŘÍ 7.V 1909-9.I 1942 * JOSEF 25.V 1874-8.X 1944 * JOSEF 11.XII 1875-JENY 18.X 1884-28.X 1944 * JIŘÍ Arnošt 7.V 1921-28.
LEO 25.XII 1922 GISELA 22.II 1902-26.X 1942 * ILKA 17.V 1907 PETR 30.III 1932-17.V 1942 * METZL Arnold 12.XI 1880 MARKÉTA 8.X 1895-2.
1887-30.IV 1942 * KAREL 14.XI 1895 ELA 13.XI 1906 MILOŠ 29.V 1933 HANUŠ 13.II 1930-23.IV 1942 * KAREL 10.V 1898-15.XII 1942 * LEO 28.XII 1890-19.
1905-JANA 17.III 1942 * MARIANA 3.X 1902 EDITA 5.X 1926 MELENA 12.V 1912-23.X 1942 * MLADA 18.IV 1915-26.IV.3 * TEREZA 21.X 1876-19.
BERTA 13.IV 1892-3.XI 1942 * MICHELOVÁ MARIE 20.X 1906-7.X 1942 * MICHELUP Teodor 26.II 1897 HEDVIKA 7.X 1891 EDITA 25.X 1932-
16.II 1895-14.VII 1942 MARKÉTA 12.III 1899-19.X 1942 FELIX 6.III 1898-19.X 1944 * MILRAD VÍTĚZSLAV 20.X 1879 IRENA 1.III 1877 OTILIE 3.VIII
ANNA 30.III 1910-20.VIII 1942 * MAINELOVÁ MARIANA? 1913-? * MINKUS E Edmund 28.XI 1881 ZDENKA 22.VII 1895 ILONA 16.III 1918 PAVLÍNA 19.
MIRSKY Evžen 12.X 1896-17.V 1942 * LEO 10.IV 1860-25.IX 1943 MELITA 27.VIII 1894-23.X 1944 * LUDMILA 27.XII 1897-6.IX 1943 * MISCHKONIG
III 30.VI 1909 SÁRA 23.X 1932-23.IV 1942 * MADKOVÁ BERTA 11.V 1885-26.X 1942 * MODRÝ JOSEF 21.VII 1900 18.V 1944 MA 13.III 1868-5.XII 1942 * MOELLE
18.X 1942 * ZIKMUND 17.V 1887 ADÉLA 16.I 1890 KATEŘINA 1.III 1923-8.IX 1942 * MA 17.VII 1874-21.XII 1942 * MOLDAUER JOSEF 12.III 1874 CECILIE 22.X
178-15.X 1942 * EVŽEN 29.VII 1891-28.IV 1942 * LAURA 15.II 1879-25.X 1942 * KONSTANCA 12.VI 1875-8.IX 1943 * MØLLEROVÁ HERMÍNA 3.I 1884-11.III 1942 * MARIE 15.I
67-15.X 1942 * JOSEF 24.XII 1894-28.IX 1944 * TEREZIE 15.II 1874-26.IV 1942 * KAREL 23.X 1877 IDA 20.VII 1876 HANA 28.IV 1912 * LEOPOLD IV.XI 1885 ANNA 27
E 30.VI 1951-28.IV 1942 * ADÉLA 17.XI 1899-23.X 1942 IRMA 4.IV 1894-23.X 1942 IRMA 6.VI 1883-23.IV 1942 * MARIE 22.V 1900 RŮŽENA 12.II 1899
5.XI 1942 * KAMILA 20.IX 1884-15.II 1942 * OSKAR 17.XI 1889-23.X 1942 * OTA 4.XI 1879 BERTA 23.X 1884 JINDŘIŠKA 21.IX 1919-4.VIII 1942 * MORBERGE
IŠKA 23.V 1908-17.V 1942 TEREZA 28.III 1868-22.X 1942 * BERNARD 26.X 1889 BERTA 23.VII 1905-15.XI 1942 * EGON 17.X 1897 ELISA 28.IX
4.XI 1880-28.X 1942 * SAMUEL 11.VI 1878-15.II 1942 * MELANIE 28.II 1878-22.X 1942 * OLGA 19.II 1870-9.X 1942 * MORWAYOVÁ ZDENKA 26.V
A 2.XII 1885-20.III 43 * HILDEGARDA 2.XI 1866-29.V 1942 * MOSEROVÁ Augusta 20.VII 1867-21.IV 1942 * RŮŽENA 8.V 1908-17.V 1942 * MOSCHELES VILÉM 30.
ÍKOVÁ ALICE 16.X 1903-29.X 1942 * MOTYKOVIČOVÁ CHARLOTA 15.XI 1917-6.IX 1942 * MOUČKOVÁ HERTA 1.X 1913-20.IX 1943 * SA
UHLSTEIN EMIL 19.III 1872-15.X 1942 * HUGO 15.VI 1877 ALICE 13.IV 1880-28.X 1944 * JINDŘICH 23.II 1871-10.VIII 1942 * AMÁLIE 13.VIII 1871-19.X
84-23.IV 1942 * JANA 31.V 1865-19.IX 1943 * IDA 15.IV 1891-18.XII 1943 * JULIE 8.VIII 1864-25.VIII 1942 * LAURA 20.X 1869-15.X 1942 * LOUISA 20.X 1882-7.I
11 39-4.IV 1942 * EMIL 6.IX 1890-9.I 1942 * ERVÍN 27.VIII 1899 MARTA 12.I 1913-6.IX 1943 * FERDINAND 25.XII 1869-19.VII 1942 * OLGA 15.VIII 1877-11.III 1943 * GUST
OFIE 13.VIII 1891-15.X 1942 * Jaroslav 25.VIII 1885-21.X 1943 * JIŘÍ 21.XII 1911-18.X 1944 * JULIUS 19.III 1877-23.X 1942 * JULIUS 6.VIII 1878-13.X 1943 * KA
K 1.X 1944 * OSVALD 12.X 1891 PAVLA 21.X 1917 JIŘÍ 20.V 1932 ZUZANA 26.IV 1939-26.X 1942 * OTA 3.X 1886-20.VIII 1944 * OTA 23.XI 1894-23.X 1944 * ADÉLA 20.X 1880 ELSA 25.X 1908
11.III 1887-22.X 1944 * EMILIE 26.V 1877-19.X 1942 * EVŽEN 11.VII 1894-25.VIII 1942 * FRANTIŠKA 28.I 1861-19.X 1942 * HANA 27.IX 1870-31.XII 1942 * H
29.XII 1910-31.XII 1942 * LOTA 18.VIII 1912-10.V 1944 * MALVÍNA 31.X 1891 GERTRUDA 9.XII 1919-6.IX 1943 * MARIE 15.II 1877-31.X 1942 * MARIE 31.V 188
25.IV 1942 * ZDENKA 9.V 1893-18.III 1943 * ZDENKA 15.III 1855-13.VIII 1942 * ZOFIE 28.VIII 1890-26.X 1942 * MUND MORIC 3.IX 1867-7.VII 1942 * A
DITA 17.X 1913-23.X 1942 JINDŘICH 21.X 1912-25.IX 1944 * AUGUSTIN 9.VIII 1867 OLGA 23.IV 1883-15.X 1942 * ERICH 21.III 1906-28.X 1944 * EVŽEN 21.I 1879-
MARTA 12.III 1906-28.II 1942 * JOSEF 12.XII 1911-6.IX 1943 * KAREL 2.IV 1855-15.X 1942 * LUDVÍK 16.III 1915-25.VIII 1942 * MAX 12.IV 1880 BOŽENA
RUDOLF 16.II 1874 VILEMÍNA 9.X 1881-19.X 1942 * RUDOLF 18.III 1871 OLGA 14.I 1898-15.X 1942 * ALŽBĚTA 10.VIII 1891 JAN 13.V 1895 MARTA 12.V 1897-26.
6.IX 1943 * LINA 22.VIII 1867-19.X 1942 * LUDMILA 12.X 1871-12.XI 1944 * STELA 28.VIII 1904 STĚPÁNKA 31.V 1954-25.IV 1942 * MUNORY KAREL 28.X 1873 MARIE
ZA ZDENKA 15.III 1895-26.IV 1942 * MUŻKOVÁ IRENA 1.XI 1900-16.IV 1942 * MYLER JOY 20.X 1894 LOLA 9.I 1904 TOMÁŠ 2.XI 1941-12.V 1944 * MYSKA ARNO
OVÁ BERTA 17.III 1884 FRANTIŠKA 2.XI 1879-6.IX 1943 * MAREK 10.III 1859-19.X 1942 * RUDOLF 4.VIII 1903-26.III 1943 * KURT 6.IV 19
X 31.XII 1890-10.VII 1942 * NACHMANN HERMAN 8.II 1878-15.X 1942 BEDŘIŠKA 22.VI 1891-26.X 1942 * FRANTIŠEK 9.X 1921-6.IX 1943 * N
O CEDEON 15.X 1913 HEDVIKA 23.VIII 1913-22.IV 1942 * NALOS 2.III 1935-6.IX 1942 * PAVEL 7.XII 1892-15.IV 19
NATH BEDŘICH 4.X 1881 ERNA 5.III 1889-6.IX 1943 * NATHAN Bernd 27.VII 1904-28.IX 1944 * EDUARD 28.IV 1874 EMILIE 28.V 1878-15.X 1942 * EMIL 2
7.IV 1942 * REGINA 27.VI 1867-23.X 1942 * EMIL 2.IX 1942 * MARKÉTA 20.III 1894-12.VII 1942 * IRMA 15.XII 1882-18.V 1944 * JANKA 4.VII 1888-25.VIII 1942
1942 * NEJEDLA IRMA 10.V 1911-? * NELAN HARY 3.XI 1912 JEANE 1.VII 1900-6.IX 1943 * NEMCOVÁ JOSEFA 4.XI 1910-26.IV 3 * NEM
4-11.V 1942 VIKTORIE 14.III 1876-4.IV 1942 * VIKTOR 17.II 1900-15.XII 1942 * ELSA 15.V 1897-28.IV 1942 * IRENA 29.X 1890-2.VIII 1942 * KAREL 23.X 1942 * NEF
TEL ADOLF 2.XI 1886-3.XI 1942 * ARTUR 14.VIII 1875 JINDŘIŠKA 12.VII 1874-15.X 1942 * BOHDAN 3.VI 1880 LILY 30.VIII 1878-19.X 1942 * EVŽEN 21.XI 1899 1
1942 MARIE 19.IV 1879-21.X 1942 * ARNOŠT 17.IV 1922-8.III 1942 * ARTUR 14.V 1881 ALVÍNA 12.III 1888-15.X 1942 * BENO 19.IX 1896 MIREK 4.IV 1924-29.V
1887-23.XI 1942 * LAURA 10.VIII 1872-19.X 1942 * MARIE 25.XII 1886-15.XI 1942 * OLGA 10.III 1896-22.X 1942 * RŮŽENA 5.IV 1883-23.IV 1942 * VALERIE 23.X
25-23.X 1942 * NEUBAUER ARNOLD 6.XI 1871 BERTA 14.XI 1884-15.X 1942 * ARNOŠT 9.VI 1880-2.VIII 1944 * BRUNO 28.IX 1895-31.X 1942 * EMIL 30
1942 * EMA 21.III 1923-25.VIII 1942 * RICHARD 14.XI 1907 FRIEDA 23.IX 1890 STĚPÁN 15.X 1934-19.X 1942 * ROBERT 13.XI 1893-15.IV 1942 * NEUBRUNN IMRE 23.XI 1879 MARTA
19.X 1942 * KAROLINA 10.III 1872-15.X 1942 * MARKÉTA 9.V 1882-9.I 1942 * LILY 7.I 1915 PETR 17.X 1938-15.X 1942 * NEUFELDOVÁ GISELA 2.V 1890-9.XI 1942 * NEUGASSER OT
MARTA 12.VIII 1908-15.XI 1942 * TEREZIE 11.VII 1876-3.XI 1942 * NEUGEBOREN JINDŘICH 8.VIII 1895 BEDŘICH 25.VIII 1925-28.X 1944 * NE
77 MARKÉTA 21.III 1900-1.IX 1942 * NEUMANN ADOLF 1.VIII 1865-9.X 1942 * ADOLF 7.VI 1899-26.X 1942 * JIŘÍ 4.XII 1922-6.IX 1943 * ALEXANDER 9.
1937-28.VII 1942 * ARNOŠT 17.I 1902-23.II 1942 * ARTUR 24.VIII 1877 FRÍDA 26.III 1883-27.XI 1942 * BEDŘICH 17.XI 1867 OLGA 25.VIII 1876-28.X 1942 *
2D 27.VII 1917-30.IV 1942 * BOHUMIL 8.V 1907-22.XI 1942 * DESIDER 15.V 1917-23.II 1942 * EDUARD 30.XII 1875-13.IX 1942 * MARIE 17.XI 1887-6.IX 19
ERA 22.III 1919-15.II 1942 * EMIL 25.VI 1894 PAVEL 28.III 1934-8.X 1942 * EMIL 6.III 1901-10.X 1944 * EMIL 10.VIII 1890-19.X 1942 * ERVÍN 16.III 1887
AVLAT 23.V 1881-10.V 1942 * FRANTIŠEK 15.III 1917-18.X 1944 * GEJZA 6.III 1892-1.III 1942 * GUSTAV 27.VII 1867-15.X 1943 * GUSTAV 12.VII 1887
x ISIDOR 18.X 1874-14. 9.X 1942 * JAKUB 15.III 1895-9.V 1942 * JAN 14.V 1909-9.IV 1942 ELA 23.V 1909-9.V 1942 * JINDŘICH 12.III 1875-23.X 1942 * JOSEF 25.IV 188
RANTIŠKA 6.XII 1879 FRANTIŠEK 31.VIII 1907-26.X 1942 * JOSEF 12.V 1887 ELSA 9.IV 1895-15.X 1944 * JIŘÍ 14.X 1922-11.III 1942 * JOSEF 25.V 188
II 7.II 1891-15.X 1942 * KAREL 21.IX 1889 DANIELA 19.X 1911-15.X 1942 * KAREL JIŘÍ 15.II 1921-8.X 1942 * LAZAR 22.VII 1891-10.III 1942
1886 CECILIE 31.I 1886-3.XI 1942 * MAXMILIÁN 31.X 1874 ANNA 8.IV 1879-26.X 1942 * MIROSLAV 1.IX 1919-28.X 1944 * MORIC 31.XII 1867 ELEONORA 11.VIII 1870-19-
2.IV 1886 ELSA 15.III 1889 HANA 15.XI 1922-15.XII 1942 * OTA 3.III 1887 MALVÍNA 6.IX 1891-26.X 1942 * OTA 10.IV 1892 KLÁRA 6.II 1895 HANA 17.V 1926-6.IX 194
III 1872-15.X 1942 * RUDOLF 30.XI 1877 ARNOŠTKA 8.II 1880-10.VII 1942 * RUDOLF 18.IX 1895 MARKÉTA 18.II 1890-19.X 1942 * RUDOLF 21.X 1878-25.VII 1942 * RUDOLF
16.I 1907 GERTRUDA 28.VIII 1912 PETR 21.X 1936-22.IX 1942 * VALTR 13.XII 1918 PAVLÍNA 11.XI 1882-19.X 1942 * VIKTOR 31.X 1896 HEDVIKA 1.XII 1909-9.X 1942
ZDENĚK 7.II 1924-8.IX 1942 * ZIKMUND 4.XI 1899 ELIŠKA 13.VIII 1905-23.X 1942 * ALICE 31.X 1881-9.V 1942 * ALICE 13.IX 1910-10.V 1942 * ALICE 25.X 1877
-10.V 1942 * ELIŠKA 17.XI 1902-26.X 1942 * EMA 22.III 1872-7.I 1944 * EMILIE 6.VI 1864-19.X 1942 * EMMA 18.VIII 1869-21.X 1942 * JOSEF 26.IV 1
R 22.VIII 1894 HELENA 4.VII 1921 EDITA 21.X 1925-8.X 1942 * IRMA 1.VII 1891 ZDENĚK 21.X 1928-10.VII 1942 * JENY 13.VIII 1891-23.X 1944 * JULIE 28.X 19
ARTA 12.VI 1905-22.X 1942 * MATYLDA 11.I 1867-19.X 1942 * MIROSLAVA 21.IV 10-? * OLGA 23.VIII 1871-19.X 1942 * PAVLA 10.VIII 1861-9.V 1942 * REGINA
1890 JIŘÍ 5.VI 1919-9.V 1942 * IRENA 12.VIII 1908 PETR 18.V 1936-19.X 1942 * JIŘÍ 27.VIII 1917
26.X 1888-9.I 1942 * OLDŘICH 15.IV 1938-15.X 1942 * NEURATH ISIDOR 12.X 1872 ANNA 17.I 1897-23.IV 1942 * IDA 3.V 1887-6.IX
II 1887 ZDENĚK 17.VIII 1922-15.X 1942 * RUDOLF 13.XII 1882 ADÉLA 22.VIII 1888 FRANTIŠEK 15.III 1920-23.IV 1942 * ANNA 1.III 1880-26.IX 1942 *
25.XI 1876-9.I 1942 * NEUSPIEL ERICH 6.III 1910 FRANTIŠKA 5.IX 1910-17.V 1942 * NEUSTADTEL ARTUR 28.III 1873 IRENA 31.I 1892-2
ARTA 8.VII 1875-19.X 1942 * MATYLDA 12.IV 1867 OTILIE 9.III 1873 VALERIE 2.X 1875-15.X 1942 *

However derogatory, however senseless the laws were, they were spread-out like a net in order to ensnare anyone, they still allowed one to live. There were no forests, no trees, no flowers. Only music and the words of poets brought comfort to those days.

Max Opperman of Brno loved classical music passionately. He was a lawyer, but that was only a job for him. At home he played a piano until he was forced to turn it over, and he never missed a concert. He couldn't resist when they played Beethoven's Fourth. There he was recognized by a neighbour, a local German lawyer, a man whom he had seen often in court and with whom he used to chat amiably about music. This former colleague turned him in during the intermission. He was led out and turned over to the Gestapo. He died in a concentration camp. But he did get to hear Beethoven's Fourth.

BUT MINE ENEMIES ARE LIVELY, AND THEY ARE STRONG: AND THEY THAT HATE ME WRONGFULLY ARE MULTIPLIED.
-- Psalms 38:20

These were self-indulgent people who loved jewelry and gold and always wanted more and more property, and they did not like to do dirty work, they ordered that this be executed by those they had subjugated and doomed to death. And as those people tried to save their lives and the lives of their children, the masters succeeded in obtaining indispensable helpers: fear ruled these helpers' diligence: it steered them like reins, so that they served until their own bitter ends. Thus the helpers established a large office with many departments, even heralds, whom they sent around to the houses where Jews lived, proclaiming sad tidings.

On 2 April, a messenger from the Jewish religious community delivered Heřman Kraus an order regarding the handover and forced sale of jewelry. Heřman Kraus had a pearl tiepin and his wife had a broach from her mother as well as some costume jewelry. The order did not pertain to these things. They also had their wedding rings, which they did not have to turn over. After the messenger left, Heřman Kraus lay down on the couch and sighed. His wife Emilie (née Austerlitzová) cried over the sink. On 3 April a messenger came from the Jewish community with a circular announcing a prohibition against Jews riding on steamboats. Heřman Kraus sighed: he did not intend to ride on a steamboat. On 4 April a messenger from the Jewish community announced a prohibition against Jews working in the film industry. Heřman Kraus took this calmly, since he had already been fired from his job as an accountant for a timber company, and had nothing whatsoever to do with film. On the 5 and 6 April the messenger did not come, but on 7 April, he came with three prohibitions and one questionnaire instead. One order informed him of the loss of patent rights to Jews; another prohibited Jews from purchasing almonds, raisins and nuts. Heřman Kraus took these orders indifferently, but his wife cried over the sink because there would not be much to put in the Christmas cake. The questionnaire that the messenger delivered outraged Kraus, it was a tax questionnaire that was many pages long. Heřman Kraus lay on the couch and sighed. Then he broke into a rage and began pounding the walls with his fists. His wife begged him with her hands pressed together to stop, since the neighbour could well be with the Gestapo. On 8 April a messenger arrived with an order that Heřman Kraus was prohibited to raise pigeons. That wasn't so bad. It got worse on the 15 April when the messenger brought an order that stores were to limit shopping hours for Jews to 11:00–1:00, and 3:00 to 4:30. Heřman Kraus's wife cried uncontrollably and lay down on the couch. Heřman lit an expensive black-market cigarette that he had been saving for quite some time. The news from the message of 18 April was not tragic either. It was an order prohibiting Jews from using dining cars and sleepers on the railways. Since Heřman Kraus knew from another order that it was forbidden for Jews to use the railways without permission from the very highest offices, he threw it in the wastepaper basket. He took the order delivered on the next day with the same indifference; it prohibited him from entering the municipal forest. Another order had prohibited him from leaving the city limits, so he couldn't get to the forests anyway. And then an order arrived that truly was tragic—and now both of the Krauses cried. It was a ban on riding the streetcar without special workers' permits. Both the Krauses were elderly.

FOR I AM READY TO HALT,
AND MY PAIN IS CONTINUALLY BEFORE ME.
-- Psalms 38:18

1943* PAVEL 21.V 1901-6.IX 1943* VILÉM 18.V 1905-30.IV 1942* ANEŽKA 16.VI 1853-16.VIII 1942* ELEONORA 2.I 1901-26.X 1941* ELFRÍDA 10.I 1879-26.X 1942* ELS
LUDMILA 3.IV 1903-31.X 1941* MAZLIACH GABRIEL 10.XII 1898-24.XI 1944* JAQUES 18.VIII 1885-18.V 1944* MECER ERVÍN 18.VIII 1906-28.IX 1944*
60-16.VII 1942* MECHNEROVÁ FRANTIŠKA 21.V 1903-14.VIII 1942* MEIEROVÁ IDA 14.III 1888-25.V 1942 FRANTIŠKA 5.IX 1862-22.X 1942* M
44* HUGO 14.III 1913 OTA 20.X 1915-6.IX 1943* KAREL 14.XII 1891-27.III 1942* PAVEL 26.XI 1902-19.XII 1941* FRANTIŠKA 18.III 1873-21.VIII 1942* MARIE 25.XII
* FRANTIŠEK 17.VIII 1900-18.XII 1943* HUGO 21.IX 1878 ELSA 28.I 1883-15.I 1942* MAX 1.IX 1879-25.III 1943 MATYLDA 21.VI 1891 JIŘÍ 22.II 1927-6
13.I 1906 HANUŠ 17.VII 1931-8.IX 1942* MEISSEL VIKTOR 27.XI 1885 MEIA 25.VIII 1889 ILSA 10.VII 1916-15.I 1942* MEISSLOVÁ DAGMAR 27
183-23.X 1944* HEDVIKA 2.III 1877-18.V 1944* HEDVIKA 8.IX 1893-19.X 1944* MARKÉTA 6.IV 1890-16.X 1944* MEISTER EMIL 9.II 1883-29.VI 1943
942* JINDŘIŠKA 18.V 1863-9.VIII 1942* MEITNER OTA 22.I 1901-18.V 1944* VIKTOR 13.III 1885-22.X 1942* LUDMILA 14.XII 1868-7.X 1942* RŮ
8.XII 1911-18.XII 1943* MELICHAR ARTUR 12.I 1878-8.V 1943 EMA 6.IX 1887-26.X 1941* ANNA 22.VI 1883-14.VII 1942* MELIONOVÁ IRMA 29.III 1896-9.V
1942 JOSEF 7.III 1927-13.VI 1942* JOSEF 7.XII 1896-12.V 1945 MARIE 10.IX 1899-28.X 1944* VILÉM 21.IX 1915-29.IX 1944 MALVÍNA 11.III 1913-4.X 1944 ZDENKA 11.X
942* HEDVIKA 7.VIII 1897-22.IX 1942 EMILIE 21.X 1869-3.VIII 1942* MARTA 27.II 1894-6.IX 1943* MELNIK RICHARD 12.II 1886 HELENA 27.VII 1887-15.I 1942
A 11.VI 1911 JIŘÍ 10.I 1933-4.X 1944* JULIE 4.VII 1857-7.VIII 1942* ŽOFIE 26.XI 1888-15.I 1942* MENCZER EMANUEL 22.IX 1891 BERTA 11.IV 1894-15.V
20.III 1897-11.X 1941* ARTUR 24.I 1873 MARTA 30.VII 1877-19.X 1942* EDUARD 1.V 1855-10.IX 1942 RŮŽENA 20.V 1862-8.IX 1942* JOSEF 23.III 1859-15.III 19
* VIKTOR 9.III 1895-1.IX 1942* EUFROSINA 21.VI 1874-25.VIII 1942* GERTRUDA 11.VI 1904-28.IV 1942* GERTRUDA 5.VII 1907-5.X 1942* GUSTA 7.XII 1895-15.II
X 1886-4.I 1943 KAREL 7.XII 1912-3.I 1943 JINDŘICH 17.IV 1915-30.XII 1942* ŽOFIE 26.III 1869-15.X 1942* MENINGEROVÁ BARBARA 4.XII 1865-15.X
.X 1941* BERTA 24.VIII 1870-19.IV 1943* IDA 22.XII 1869-15.X 1942* VALERIE 30.VII 1893-1.IV 1942* MENZELES EMIL 28.IV 1879 ERNA 20.X 1891-28
MARTIN 30.XII 1897-3.XI 1941* HERMÍNA 15.VIII 1876 BERTA 11.V 1917-12.VII 1942* MERORY ALFRED 22.I 1885 NELA 19.IV 1891 ALŽBĚTA 21.XII
SING LEO 3.III 1883-18.I 1942 JETA 20.XII 1897-16.X 1944* RŮŽENA 20.III 1862-19.X 1942* MESSINGER HANUŠ 8.X 1899-26.I 1943* KA
OSEF 17.XII 1874 ANNA 23.VII 1879-3.XI 1941* VALTR 21.III 1903-29.IX 1944* METH BEDŘICH 22.V 1888 MARKÉTA 9.IX 1890-20.VIII 1942* JUL
ER EMIL 2.XII 1882-12.X 1944* GUSTAV 28.III 1869 ANNA 13.XII 1873-15.X 1942* JIŘÍ 27.V 1909-9.I 1942* JOSEF 25.V 1874-8.XI 1944* JOSEF 12.XII
ANKA 16.VIII 1911 EVA 29.IX 1922-6.IX 1943* METZKER LEO 25.XII 1902 GISELA 22.III 1902-26.X 1942* ILKA 19.VII 1902 PETR 30.III 1932-17.V 194
RMÍNA 2.VII 1898-6.X 1944* GUSTAV 1.IX 1879 IDA 2.VIII 1887-30.IV 1942* KAREL 14.XI 1895 ELA 3.VII 1906 MILOŠ 29.V 1933 HANUŠ 17.II 19
1907-12.XI 1942* GABRIELA 29.VII 1888-1.IX 1942* GRÉTA 17.II 1905 JANA 17.III 1905-17.V 1942* MARIANA 3.X 1902 EDITA 9.IX 1926 HELENA 12.V 1931-2
MARTIN 25.XII 1908-17.V 1942* MICHALITSCHKOVÁ BERTA 13.IV 1892-3.XI 1941* MICHELOVÁ MARIE 20.X 1906-7.XI 1942* MICHE
VÍTĚZSLAV 26.VI 1881 MARIE 1.III 1899-20.VIII 1942* HEDVIKA 16.IV 1895-14.VII 1942 MARKÉTA 12.III 1899-19.X 1942 FELIX 6.II 1901-14.VII 1942* MI
ARNO 9.XII 1897-8.IX 1942* MINDLIN SIDOR 22.VII 1895 ANNA 30.III 1910-20.VIII 1942* MINELOVÁ MARIANA ? 1923-?* MINKUS EDMU
78-15.I 1942* MIRON ISRAEL JAKUB ? 1903-31.X 1941* MIRSKY EVŽEN 12.IV 1896-17.V 1942* LEO 10.IV 1860-25.IX 1943 MELITA 27.VIII 1894-2
1.XI 1879-23.X 1944* MITTELMAN MOŘIC 10.XI 1900 VALERIE 30.VII 1909 EVA 5.IX 1932-3.XI 1941* MLÁDKOVÁ BERTA 1.VI 1885-26.X 1942* MODRÝ J
RMÍNA 28.XII 1893 MARGITA 21.IV 1928-6.IX 1943* VALTR 22.VII 1918-8.IX 1942* ZIKMUND 14.V 1887 ADÉLA 16.I 1890 KATEŘINA 1.III 1923-8.IX 1942* MATYLDA 24
89-26.X 1942 JAN 5.VII 1891-18.XII 1943* CECILIE 31.XII 1874-26.X 1942 EVŽEN 29.VIII 1891-28.IV 1942* LAURA 15.II 1879-9.X 1944* KONSTANCA 17.VI 1875-8.IX 1943
BOHUMIL 8.V 1896-?* JAKUB 6.XI 1872-8.X 1942* JOSEF 31.VII 1867-15.XII 1943* JOSEF 24.XII 1894-28.IX 1944 TEREZIE 15.I 1874-24.III 1943* KAREL 3.IX 1894 IDA 20.
1.III 1913-9.X 1944* ROBERT 12.IV 1887 HERMÍNA 31.X 1889 JULIE 30.VII 1931-28.IV 1942* ADÉLA 11.XII 1899 IDA 11.IV 1903-26.X 1942* IRMA 4.IV 1873-15.XII 1943
X 1885 GISELA 18.VIII 1892 BEDŘICH 15.XII 1914-15.I 1942* MAX 6.XI 1883-21.I 1944 KAMILA 20.IX 1884-19.X 1944* OSKAR 12.XII 1889-9.I 1942* OTA 4.II 1879 BER
VILÉM 26.IX 1905-20.VIII 1942* BEDŘICH 3.V 1897 FRANTIŠKA 23.V 1908-17.V 1942 TEREZA 28.III 1868-19.X 1942* BERNARD 24.X 1889 BERTA 2
III 1888 ANNA 9.I 1890-12.VI 1942* OTA 29.VIII 1904 PAVLA 14.XI 1880-28.IV 1942* SAMUEL 11.VI 1878-15.I 1942* MELANIE 28.III 1878-22.X 1942* O
A 17.VIII 1895 LISY 1.V 1924-15.I 1942* EVŽEN 19.V 1879 ELIŠKA 2.II 1885-20.I 1943* HILDEGARDA 20.IX 1866-29.V 1943* MOSEROVÁ AUGU
OSKOVIČ DESIDER 27.III 1905-30.IV 1942* MOSKOVITS ANDER 22.IX 1895 ALŽBĚTA 25.III 1900-30.IV 1942* RŮŽENA 8.V 1908-17.V
20.VIII 1942* MALVÍNA 30.XII 1904-17.V 1942* MOTYČKOVÁ ALICE 26.XII 1903-29.X 1942* MOTYOVIČOVÁ CHARLOTA 18.I 1917-
22.X 1942* MUDROVÁ KLÁRA 10.XI 1894-26.X 1942* MUHLSTEIN EMIL 19.III 1872-15.X 1942* HUGO 5.VI 1877 ALICE 12.IV 1883-28.X 1944*
SLAV 10.VII 1871 HEDVIKA 15.I 1876-15.X 1942* ELSA 18.X 1884-21.X 1941* JANA 31.V 1865-19.IX 1943 IDA 15.IV 1891-18.XII 1943* JULIE 14.VIII 1864-25
UELLER MAXIMILIÁN 25.X 1881-25.VIII 1942* MÜLLER ALFRED 15.II 1876-21.X 1941 ELA 18.XII 1886-11.II 1942 HANUŠ 19.X 1907-31.VIII 1942* A
1904 RUTH 11.X 1932-21.X 1941* EMIL 2.VIII 1884 IDA 11.VIII 1889-4.VIII 1942* EMIL 6.XII 1890-9.I 1942* ERVÍN 27.VIII 1899 MARTA 12.I 1913-6.IX 1943* FERD
A 7.IX 1922 JIŘÍ 8.I 1927-1.IX 1942* HUGO 19.IX 1891-6.IX 1943 ŽOFIE 13.VIII 1891-15.V 1944* JAROSLAV 29.III 1885-21.X 1941* JIŘÍ 21.XII 1914-18.XII 1943* J
ŘIC 20.VII 1877 HERMÍNA 2.X 1882-31.X 1941* MOŘIC 11.I 1887-1.X 1944* OSVALD 12.X 1891 PAVLA 21.VI 1907 JIŘÍ 20.VI 1932 ZUZANA 26.IV 1939-26.X 194
OLF 2.X 1893-22.X 1942* SALOMON 20.XI 1860 JENY 29.VIII 1865-19.X 1942* SAMUEL 19.X 1873 KAROLÍNA 4.III 1879 BEDŘICH 18.III 1912-22.X 1942* VIK
* ELA 31.I 1893-20.VIII 1942* ELISA 30.V 1893-21.X 1941* ELSA 11.III 1887-30.IV 1942* EMILIE 26.V 1877-19.X 1942* EVŽENIE 11.VIII 1894-25.VIII 1942* FRAN
* LILY 24.II 1895-18.V 1944 MIMI 9.IV 1921-20.I 1943* LILY 29.XII 1910-11.XI 1942* LOTA 18.VIII 1912-10.VI 1942* MALVÍNA 31.X 1891 GERTRUDA 9.XII
379-1.IX 1942* TEREZIE 5.V 1892-26.X 1942* TRUDA 2.X 1901-23.X 1944 ZDENĚK 4.V 1893-18.III 1943* ZDEŇKA 25.II 1855-13.VIII 1942* ŽOFIE 28.VIII
371-15.X 1942* MUNK ARNOŠT 17.III 1905-29.IX 1944 EDITA 17.IX 1913 JINDŘICH 21.XI 1942-23.X 1944* AUGUSTIN 9.VIII 1867 OLGA 23.IV 188
VALTR 4.II 1924 HERBERT 2.V 1926-15.I 1942* JOSEF 21.XI 1893 MARTA 22.III 1906 JIŘÍ 17.I 1927-1.IX 1942* JOSEF 12.XI 1911-6.IX 1943* KAREL 2.IV 1855-13.
6-29.III 1942* RICHARD 4.III 1877 HEDVIKA 4.V 1882-9.V 1942* RUDOLF 16.X 1871 VILEMÍNA 9.X 1881-19.X 1942* RUDOLF 26.VI 1885 OLGA 14.I 1898-15.
2-15.I 1942* JULIE 23.VII 1889-20.I 1943* KAROLINA 13.IV 1871-15.X 1942* LINA 2.VI 1861-19.X 1942* LUDMILA 12.XI 1891-12.XII 1943* STELA 28.VII 1904 ŠTĚPÁN
RANTIŠEK 25.XI 1905 GISELA 10.V 1897-8.X 1942* KAREL 29.V 1911-6.IX 1943* OTA ? 1912-31.XII 1941* MARTA 11.V 1908-26.X 1942* PAVLA 1.VI 1875-15.XII 1943* MU
1922-15.III 1945* BOHUMÍR 9.VIII 1887-26.VIII 1943* MUŽÁKOVÁ ZDEŇKA 15.I 1893-28.IX 1944* MUŽKOVÁ IRENA 1.XI 1900-14.VII 1942* MYLER JOY 20
1942* NADEL JOSEF 7.II 1903-?* NADELFEST FILIP 3.III 1854-19.X 1942* HANUŠ 20.XI 1904 FRANTIŠKA 2.XI 1879-6.IX 1943* MAREK 10.II
-18.XII 1943* OTILIE 17.III 1861-24.II 1943* NAGELBERGOVÁ BERTA 17.III 1884 MARTA 1.IX 1907-6.IX 1943* NAGELFESTOVÁ RŮŽEN
2.V 1942 KAREL 8.XII 1919-24.IV 1942* NACHHÄUSER MAX 31.XII 1890-10.VI 1942* NACHMANN HEŘMAN 8.II 1878-7.VI 1942 BEDŘIŠKA 22.VI 1891-26.
KOVÁ MARGITA 13.XII 1913-6.IX 1943* NARCISSENFELD GEDEON 15.X 1913 HEDVIKA 23.VIII 1919-27.IV 1942* NARZISSENFELDOVÁ SÁRA 12.I
N HUGO 2.XI 1897 HARIETA 23.XI 1894 JUTA 15.III 1921-3.XI 1941* NATH BEDŘICH 4.IV 1881 ERNA 13.VI 1895-6.IX 1943* NATHAN BERND 7.VIII 1904-28.IX 1
VOJTĚCH 20.IV 1883 BERTA 24.XI 1885 OLGA 26.IX 1925-8.IX 1942* EMILIE 6.IX 1890-6.IX 1943 JIŘÍ 15.IX 1915-9.V 1942* IRMA 15.IX 1882-18.V 1944*
1933-30.IV 1942* NAVRÁTILOVÁ ANNA 14.X 1897-26.X 1942* NAWRATOVÁ MARKÉTA 20.II 1894-12.VI 1942* NEFELES ARTUR 26.
ERLE 27.VIII 1860-6.X 1942* NEINER ARNOŠT 27.V 1897-1.IX 1942* NEJEDLÁ IRMA 10.V 1911-?* NELAN HARY 3.XII 1912 JEANETA 11.III 1920-6.
2* NESTLEROVÁ MARKÉTA 25.II 1875-26.X 1941* NETTEL ADOLF 2.XI 1886-3.XI 1941* ARTUR 1.VIII 1875 JINDŘIŠKA 12.VII 1874-15.X 1942* B
-15.XII 1943 VIKTOR 5.VI 1906-6.IX 1943* RICHARD 24.X 1874-11.IV 1943 VIKTORIE 14.III 1876-4.I 1943* VIKTOR 17.XII 1900-15.XII 1943* ELSA 15.V 1887-9
1.VII 1896 MILAN 24.VI 1924-18.V 1944* ARNOŠT 22.I 1877-7.VIII 1942 MARIE 19.IV 1879-21.X 1941* ARNOŠT 17.I 1922-8.III 1945* ARTUR 14.V 1881 MALVÍN
A 11.IV 1888-14.VII 1942* MAXMILIÁN 10.III 1870 OLGA 25.VIII 1875-19.X 1942* OTA 8.XI 1874-19.X 1943* OTA 3.III 1894-19.V 1943* RICHARD 17.I 1908-2
1871-19.X 1942* GABRIELA 5.IX 1892-9.I 1942* HEDVIKA 25.IV 1887-3.XI 1941* LAURA 10.III 1872-19.X 1942* MARIE 25.III 1886-15.XII 1943* OLGA 10.II
UBACH JAKUB 12.XI 1902-20.I 1943* ELIŠKA 15.VIII 1905-23.V 1942* NEUBAUER ARNOLD 6.III 1871 BERTA 1.II 1884-15.X 1942* ARNOŠT
.XI 1942* OSKAR 23.III 1880-25.VIII 1942 PAVEL 27.III 1885-17.VII 1942* OTA 24.II 1923-25.VIII 1942* RICHARD 14.IX 1907 FRIEDA 23.VII 1909 ŠTĚPÁN 15.
904 RUTH 18.VII 1928-20.I 1943* MATYLDA 13.X 1881-9.X 1944* NEUBERGOVÁ ADÉLA 28.V 1882-25.VIII 1942* LILY 21.VI 1915 PETR 17.X 19
86 MARKÉTA 28.IX 1896-6.IX 1943* RICHARD 31.VIII 1872-19.X 1942* KAROLINA 10.III 1872-15.X 1942* MARKÉTA 9.V 1882-9.I 1942* NEUFELD
5-30.IV 1942* LEOPOLD 1.X 1879 RŮŽENA 5.X 1881-8.X 1942* MARTA 12.VII 1908-4.VIII 1942* TEREZIE 21.VII 1876-3.XI 1941* NEUGEBOREN J
NA 31.X 1865-9.III 1943* NEULÄNDER ARTUR 24.VI 1897 MARKÉTA 12.II 1900-1.IX 1942* NEUMANN ADOLF 1.VIII 1865-9.X 1942* ADOLF
ARNOŠT 18.III 1894-9.I 1942* ARNOŠT 22.VIII 1898 EVA 20.X 1937-28.VII 1942* ARNOŠT 17.I 1902-9.III 1945* ARTUR 24.VII 1877 FRÍDA 26.III 1883-27.
1.VII 1915-9.V 1942* BEDŘICH 12.XI 1924-8.II 1945* BERNARD 29.VI 1912-30.IV 1942* BOHUMIL 8.V 1907-22.VIII 1943* DESIDER 15.V 1917-3.XI 1941*
3* EMIL 6.X 1881 ANTONIE 30.I 1884 MARIE 11.XII 1914 VĚRA 2.III 1919-15.I 1942* EMIL 25.X 1894 PAVEL 28.III 1934-8.X 1942* EMIL 6.III 1904-
FRANTIŠEK 6.X 1907-18.V 1944* FRANTIŠEK 23.IV 1915 PAVLA 13.IV 1881-10.VI 1942* FRANTIŠEK 15.III 1917-18.XII 1943* GEJZA 6.III 1892-1.I
1890 EMA 9.III 1889-9.V 1942* HUGO 28.III 1913-18.XII 1943* ISIDOR 18.IX 1874-14.X 1943* JAKUB 15.III 1895-9.V 1942* JAN 14.V 1909-9.V 19
RUTH 12.III 1924-8.IX 1942* JOSEF 23.VII 1879-9.VII 1942 FRANTIŠKA 6.XI 1879 FRANTIŠEK 31.VIII 1907-26.X 1941* JOSEF 12.IV 1887 ELSA 9.IV 18
2 OLGA 29.V 1897-14.VII 1942* KAREL 10.V 1883-9.V 1942* KAREL 21.II 1893-8.X 1942* KAREL 28.XI 1902-?* KAREL 19.XI 1911 DANIELA IVA 30.XI 1942-18.XII 19
3.X 1875-19.X 1942* LUDVÍK 11.IV 1873-19.X 1942* MAREK 28.I 1886 CECILIE 18.III 1886-3.XI 1941* MAXMILIÁN 23.V 1874 ANNA 8.IV 1879-26.X 1942* MIROSLA
3* OSKAR 2.IX 1900-16.XII 1941* OTA 4.III 1883-10.VI 1942* OTA 2.IV 1886 ELSA 15.III 1889 HANA 15.XII 1922-25.VIII 1942* OTA 13.XII 1887 MALVÍNA 6.X 1891-26
XII 1880-26.IV 1944 MARIANA 18.VII 1925-6.IX 1943* RUDOLF 23.II 1872-15.X 1942* RUDOLF 30.I 1877 ARNOŠTKA 8.III 1880-10.VI 1942* RUDOLF 13.IX 1877 M
R 28.VII 1866-1.VIII 1942 PAVLÍNA 10.V 1877-15.X 1942* VALTR 16.I 1907 GERTRUDA 28.VIII 1912 PETR 11.X 1936-22.IX 1942* VALTR 13.XII 1918 PAVLÍNA 11.II
1900-23.X 1944* VOJTĚCH 23.XI 1898 ANTONÍN 1.IV 1928-9.V 1942* ZDENĚK 11.I 1924-8.IX 1942* ZIKMUND 4.VI 1861-15.X 1942* ADÉLA 22.IV 1878-9.V 1942* ALICE 2
1942* ELA 21.X 1905 JANA 18.I 1939-28.X 1944* ELIŠKA 23.IV 1893-10.VI 1942* ELIŠKA 1.VII 1902-26.X 1941* ELSA 22.IV 1884-9.I 1942* EMA 22.I 1871-2.I 1944* EMI
9.IV 1904-10.VI 1942* HANA 12.VIII 1911 PETR 6.VI 1934-19.X 1944* HEDVIKA 25.VII 1909-30.IV 1942 LILY 25.X 1934-23.X 1944* HELENA 3.X 1869-15.
1 31.VIII 1925-8.IX 1942* IRMA 29.V 1891-9.V 1942* IRMA 22.XI 1894 HELENA 4.VI 1921 EDITA 21.X 1925-8.X 1942* IRMA 1.I 1907 ZDENĚK 21.X
TA 2.VIII 1895-27.IX 1942 ERNA 25.IX 1902-20.VIII 1942* MARTA 12.VI 1905-9.I 1942* MATYLDA 1.I 1867-19.X 1942* MIROSLAVA ? 1940-?* OLGA
84 MARTA 7.VII 1889-16.X 1941* PAVEL 10.IV 1889 LILY 5.I 1890 JIŘÍ 5.VI 1919-6.IX 1943* IRENA 12.VIII 1908 PETR 18.V 1943-16.X 1944* NEU
5 ANNA 9.III 1910-23.X 1944* MARIE ?-?* PAVLA 26.X 1888-9.I 1942 OLDŘICH 15.IV 1938-15.XII 1943* NEURATH ISIDOR 23.
1895-? ELA ? 1910-?* HUGO 4.XII 1885 PAVLA 26.III 1887 ZDENĚK 17.VIII 1924-6.IX 1943* RUDOLF 13.XII 1882 ADÉLA 22.VIII 1891 FRA
TIŠKA 8.VII 1913-6.IX 1943* HEŘMAN 6.VIII 1881 OTILIE 5.XI 1876-9.V 1942* NEUSPIEL ERICH 26.I 1910 FRANTIŠKA 5.IX 1910-17.V 1942
* ADÉLA 9.VIII 1887-25.VIII 1942* IRENA 24.I 1897-1.IV 1942* MARTA 8.VII 1875-19.X 1942* MATYLDA 12.IV 1862 OTILIE 9.II 1873 VALERIE 7.X 1875-15.X
3.VI 1936-9.III 1943* RUDOLF 4.IV 1886 HELENA 13.III 1898-16.X 1944 VĚRA 2.V 1923-18.XII 1943 MILOŠ 8.VI 1927-19.X 1944* FRANTIŠKA 15.VIII 1868-
R 4.VIII 1896 HELENA 17.I 1897-6.IX 1943* SAMUEL 14.VII 1903-18.XII 1943* NIEWELTOVÁ EMA 20.III 1898-23.I 1943* NIMHÄUSER LEO
VIII 1894-20.I 1943* LUDVÍK 7.VI 1858-27.VII 1942 ANNA 18.IX 1869-15.XII 1943* MAX 16.XII 1890-17.VI 1943* OTA 2.II 1880 ERNESTINA 1.VII 1890
2* NORDMANNOVÁ CHAJA 14.VII 1898-9.I 1942* NORMAN KURT 16.X 1918-28.IX 1944* NOSOVÁ HERMÍNA 13.V 1883-
ARNOŠT 15.IX 1877 ALŽBĚTA 8.III 1892-6.IX 1943* ERVÍN 13.VIII 1891 IRMA 15.XII 1901 JOSEF 25.X 1931-18.V 1944* HUGO 31.I 1886 MARI

GERTRUDA 7.1916-9.* GERTRUDA 15.VIII.1937-9.III.1943 VĚRA 13.VII.1937-6.X.1943* HEDVIKA 22.X.1904-6.X.1943* IRMA 17.I.1889-14.VII.1942* KLÁRA 6.X.8.XI.1902-28.XI.1943* MILADA 25.IX.1895-17.XII.1944* MEDÁKOVÁ EVA 15.II.1901-11.III.1942* MEEROVÁ ELA 10.VI.1883 ALŽBĚTA 14.III.1914-28.I.XANDER 30.X.XII.1881-9.III.1942* MEISEL ADOLF 31.V.1880 BEDŘIŠKA 15.I.1888-6.IX.1943* ALFRÉD 14.IV.1879 LOTKA 17.V.1891 JAN 5.III.1914-13.X.5.X.1871-15.X.1942* HELENA 18.III.1937-10.VI.1942* KAROLA 2.I.1895-28.IV.1942* ROZÁLIE 14.III.1856-23.IV.1942* RŮŽENA 15.X.1874-15.XII.1943* AAI MEISSNER ARNOŠT 26.VI.1904-15.III.1943* ARTUR 29.X.1881-19.X.1944* EMIL 27.V.1893-1.XIV.3* JAKUB 31.I.1883-16.XI.1943* JINDŘICH 18.KAR 10.X.1902-6.XII.1942* MEISTERLES ARNOŠT 20.X.1893-17.X.1943 IRMA 2.5.X.1893-18.XII.1943* HUGO 23.X.1899 FRANTIŠKA 1.III.1894-1.III.1943 FI BERT 21.1890 OLGA 13.VI.1897-6.IX.1943* GUSTAV 23.VI.1881-17.III.1942* MEIXNER OTA 2.X.1887 ANNA 7.III.1891 HELENA 26.X.1920-1.III.1943* HAN 7.III.1943-8.X 194.x.ANNA 30.X.1868-15.X.1942* HEDVIKA 7.I.1869-19.X.1942* HERMÍNA 26.X.1863-15.X.1942* HILDA 4.X.1896-12.XII.1942* OLGA 7.XII.1816-9* M58-26.X.1942* MELZER AUGUSTIN 12.VIII.1903 HERTA 20.I.1905 HARY 11.III.1930 MARIE EVA 2.I.1931 HANA 31.III.1934-26.X.1942* BENJAMIN 15.III.1936* FRANTIŠEK 8.III.1921 16.V.1944* MENDEL ALFRED 28.V.1886-26.X.1943 VILÉM 31.V.1879-15.XII.1943* KATEŘINA 5.VI.1895-4.VIII.1942* MENDE 1868-1.III.1942* KAREL 2.II.1885 IRMA 19.X.1894-16.X.1944* KAREL 2.9.X.1893 JIŘÍ 2.V.1925-13.III.1944* KAREL 21.III.1898-29.IX.1944* MARTA 24.V.1897 M V.1859-22.X.1942* IDA 6.XI.1866-23.X.1942* JOSEFINA 23.I.1877-22.X.1942* IDA 11.VIII.1879-26.X.1942* HERTA 28.VIII.1911-14.V.1944* JOSEFA 20.ARNOŠT 29.VIII.1889-21.X.1943* MENZEL FRANTIŠEK 31.XII.1877 ELSA 21.X.1900-28.X.1944* HERMAN 14.VIII.1886-14.VII.1942* JULIUS 13.X.1891 ALŽBĚT ER ERVIN 7.1906-2* MERKSAMER JOSEF 4.XII.1877 ELSA 27.X.1944* SIMON 13.X.1874-15.XII.1943* MILADA 21.X.1903 JIŘÍ 31.III.1917-19-19.712-28.IV.194* MERTEN FELIX 11.IX.1876-8.VIII.1944* AMALIE 28.VIII.1886-4.VIII.1942* MERTENS ARTUR 2.IX.1886 MARIE 27.III.1905-17.15.I.1942* MESSNER EMANUEL 5.XI.1897-28.XI.1944* HELENA 11.XI.1874-6.X.1944* MESSINGOVÁ MATYLDA 7.X.1853-3.X.1942* PETR 5.V.1930-6.X.1942*B.RTA 27.III.1893 LEO 23.V.1875-11.XI.1921-15.XII.1943* PETR OSVALD 23.X.1913-18.XII.1943* METTELOVÁ ELIŠKA 27.V.1893 GERTRUDA 6.I.1924-B 884-28.X.1944* JIŘÍ ARNOŠT 19.V.1921-28.XII.1943* JOSEF 21.V.1923-6.X.1943* KAREL 24.III.1891-21.X.1942* OTA 22.III.1891-18.XII.1943*E EMILIE 29.NOLD 17.X.1880 MARKÉTA 8.XII.1922-21.XII.1942* PAVEL 24.III.1923-6.IX.1943* ARNOŠT 21.V.1902 ALŽBĚTA 10.XI.1REI 10.IV.1898-15.XII.1943* LEO 28.XII.1903 ALENA 18.VII.1935-15.XII.1943* LUDVÍK 7.IV.1859-7.VII.1942* MATYLDA 7.VI.1854-24.VII.1942* MAJ 18.IV.1915-26.XII.1943* TEREZA 21.X.1876-19.XII.1942* MEYER HANUŠ 31.III.1877-28.X.1942* HERBERT 3.II.1909-26.X.1944* MAJ 1877 HEDVIKA 9.X.1891 EDITA 25.XII.1917-28.X.1944* TOMÁŠ 23.III.1933-20.I.1943* FLORA 3.III.1867-15.X.1942* OTTILIE 24.III.1893-17.V.194* MEYERHARDTOVÁ FI 1877 HEDVIKA 9.X.1891 EDITA 25.XII.1917-28.X.1944* TOMÁŠ 23.III.1933-20.I.1943* FLORA 3.III.1867-15.X.1942* OTTILIE 24.III.1893-17.V.194* MAICH KA 22.VIII.1895 ILONA 16.III.1898 PAVLÍNA 19.III.1903-3.XII.1943* JOSEF 22.IX.1891-24.V.1944* IRMA 25.VI.1895-23.X.1944* KURT 29.III.1918 SELMA 2.X.1885 72.XI.1897-6.IX.1943* MISCHKÖNIG FELIX 11.I.1899 GERTRUDA 7.IX.1903 ROBERT 30.V.1895-3.XI.1941* GRÉTA 21.III.1899-15.VII.1942* HEDVIKA 24.II.V.194x.EMA 11.1868-15.III.1944* MOELLER EMIL 28.VII.1877 12.V.1942* MOGAN ZIKMUND 26.X.1907-6.IX.1943* MOHL JOSEF 8.IV.1869-14.V.1943* H.II.HERMÍNA 3.I.1884-11.III.1942* MARTA 3.I.1881-30.VI.1942* MARTA 7.IX.1898-16.VII.1942* MOLDOVAN SALOMON 29.III.1921-26.X.1942* MOLDOVAN LAZAR 26.XII.1919-1976-18.VI.1943* LEOPOLD 14.XI.1885 ANNA 25.III.1890-18.VI.1944* MARIA 7.XII.1879-14.IX.1942* MOLAVETZ ALFRED 11.XII.1871 JINDŘICH 1.VII.1912-17.JV.1942* MARIE 22.V.1900 RŮŽENA 12.VI.1899-27.XII.1943* VALTR 3.V.1917-18.V.1942* LUDVÍK 22.I.1900 GRÉTA 13.VIII.1902* HANA SKAUZIX 1919-4.XII.1943* MORBERGEROVÁ SELMA 19.IX.1884-4.VIII.1942* MORELOVÁ MARIE 12.X.1888-1.XII.1942* VALERIE 27.V.1910-12-ECON 27.I.X.194.4 ELISA 28.IX.1902 EDITA 26.IV.1929-17.X.1944* ARNOŠT 27.V.1933-17.X.1944* ECON 3.VII.1922-23.I.1943* EMIL 16.IX.188 192* MORWAYOVÁ ZDENKA 7.V.1881-1.XII.1943* MOSAUER ANTONÍN 6.III.1873 IDA 29.V.1889-18.XII.1943* MOSCHELES VILÉM 30.XI.1861-5.III.194* IIII193* MOSCHLOVÁ HELENA 7.IX.1920-20.VIII.1942* MOŠKOVIČ ARON 12.III.1918-21.III.1943* EMERICH 22.I.1894* JINDŘICH 7.I.1912-17.I.194* OVA HELENA 7.IX.1920-20.VIII.1942* MOŠKOVIČ ARON 12.III.1918-21.III.1943* EMERICH 22.I.1894* JINDŘICH 7.I.1912-17.I.194* SARA BERTA 8.VIII.1901-25.V.1942* MOUCHOVÁ MATYLDA 7.X.1853-29.X.1942* MOWSCH 1-10.VIII.1942* AMALIE 10.VIII.1871-19.X.1942* JULIUS 2.II.1869-19.X.1942* JULIUS 20.III.1875-28.I.1942* LEO 9.X.1904-28.X.1944* FRIEDA 14.III.1899 X.1869-15.X.1942* LOUISA 20.III.1902-1.III.194* MARGITA 18.XII.1899 IMANUEL 22.VII.1929 GABRIEL 18.IX.1930 MARIE 3.III.1932-16.X.1944* AL 3.X.1942* ARNOŠT 19.VIII.1903-30.X.1942 BEDŘIŠKA 3.VI.1916-11.III.1942* BEDŘICH 25.III.1890-26.X.1944* BEDŘICH 13.X.1898-14.IX.1942 OLGA 5.XI.1874-15.IX.1942* GUSTAV 12.V.1880 MARKÉTA 12.IV.1890-18.IX.1942* HANUŠ 12.IV.1890-28.X.1944* HERTA 26.III.1919-6.IX.1943* FI JULIUS 14.VIII.1878-18.V.1944* KAREL 7.IV.1883 MARKÉTA 23.X.1882 NINA 22.XII.1918-15.XII.1943* KAREL ANTONÍN 30.V.1901-21.IV.1945* LÍZA 31.V.194.5* ADÉLA 20.X.1880 ELSA 25.XI.1908-4.VIII.1942* ALOISIE 24.X.1877-15.X.1942* ALŽBĚTA 19.VIII.1876 KAREL 18.VII.1900-3.X.1941* ANNA 22.VIII.187-X.194.7* HANA 27.XI.1920-31.XII.1942* HEDVIKA 24.XII.1873-15.X.1942* HEDVIKA 26.X.1887-28.IV.1947* HEDVIKA 7.X.1890-26.X.1942* IDA 22.III.18 ARIE 15.III.1877-21.V.1944* MARIE 31.V.1883 HANA 9.IX.1921 MILADA 5.XII.1919-26.X.1942* MELANIE 20.1883-28.XII.1944* MILADA 7.VI.1915-HA UND MORIC 3.IV.1867-27.VII.1942* MUNDSTEINOVÁ HERMÍNA 11.IX.1896-15.III.1942* MUNELES FRANTIŠEK 24.V.1896 KAROLINA CH 7.XI.III.1904-28.X.1944* EVŽEN 21.III.1897-31.VII.1942* RUTH 23.XI.1906-21.X.1943* FRANTIŠEK 8.IV.1890-9.I.1942* GUSTAV 7.V.1907-6.IX.1943* HANU 7.1891 IDA 11.V.1895 MARTA 17.V.1897-26.X.1942* ANNA 10.XI.1867-15.X.1942* ANNA 14.XII.1881-18.XII.1943* ELSA 31.VII.1902-25.IV.194* MILAN 6.IV.1919-25.I V.194* MUNORY KAREL 28.X.1873 MARIE 11.VII.1883 BEDŘICH 21.XII.1908-18.V.1944* ROBERT 14.VIII.1880-21.VII.1942* ELSA 14.IV.1882 GISELA 15.VIII.1880-15.III.194* K 25.XI.1895 MARKÉTA 16.IV.1892-17.V.1944* HUGO 21.IV.1863-19.X.1942* KAROLÍNA 6.V.1868-23.VII.1942* KAREL 5.VI.1885 OLGA 5.XI.1887-12.VII.1942* OSKAR RUDOLF 4.VIII.1903-26.VI.1943* KURT 6.IV.1913 HELENA 11.I.1889-31.V.1947* FRANTIŠEK 26.VIII.1863-22.VII.1942* JOSEF 1.II.1900-28.X.1944* ANNA 18.VII.18 7.IV.1921 ARNOŠT 11.IX.1921-6.IX.1942* NAGELSTOCK BEDŘICH 30.V.1910-24.II.1945* LOUIS 4.XII.1865-25.V.1942* EMIL 7.III.1866-12.X.14 IRI 24.VI.1933-6.IX.1943* PAVEL 21.II.1892-15.V.1944* RUDOLF 10.XII.1872-15.XII.1943* JENY 21.III.1883-15.V.1944* LOUIS 12.IV.1908-18.V.1944* ARNOŠTKA 31.III.1878-24-30.I.1942* NASCHMANN MARIE 21.V.1885-6.X.194* NASS FRANTIŠEK 23.XII.1877-12.V.1942* HUGO 27.VI.1877-13.VII.1943* ERNA 10.III.1888-6.IX.1943* JOSEF 28.VI.1907 HEDVIKA 1874 EMILIE 29.IV.1878-15.XII.1942* EMIL 23.III.1912-6.III.1945* HUGO 27.VI.1877-13.VII.1943* ERNA 10.III.1888-6.IX.1943* JOSEF 28.VI.1907 HEDVIKA 1874 EMILIE 29.IV.1878-15.XII.1942* EMIL 23.III.1912-6.III.1945* HUGO 27.VI.1877-13.VII.1943* ERNA 10.III.1888-6.IX.1943* JOSEF 28.VI.1907 HEDVIKA S.VIII.1943* REGINA 22.VI.1867-15.X.1942* NATHANSEN HERBERT 12.XI.1899-30.VI.1944* NATSCHERADETZ EGON 25.I.1899 EVA 28.I.8 ADÉLA 18.VII.1878 ALOISIE 17.V.1893-30.V.1942* KAMILA 13.V.1881-25.VII.1942* NEFOVÁ GERTRUDA 21.VI.1898-9.X.1944* NEIGER MORK OVA JOSEFA 15.XI.1870-26.I.1943* NĚMEČKOVÁ ESTER 10.VIII.1898-14.V.1944* NEMIROVSKY ALEXANDER 17.VI.1896 HELENA 29.VI.1903 JAN ILY 10.VII.1878-19.XII.1943* EVŽEN 27.II.1890-2.III.1941* EMILIE 18.VIII.1892-6.IX.1943* GUSTAV 14.VIII.1896-19.XII.194* JAN 6.VII.1882 PIROŠKA 23.VIII.1904-24.II.1890-2.VIII.1942* KAREL 21.XII.1896* EVŽEN 3.VII.1912-3.XII.1941* IRMA 14.VIII.1887 MARTA 23.IX.1889-26.III.1943* KATEŘINA 25.IX.1889-26.III.1943* LYDIA 1.III.1893-21.IV.194* P4.X.BENO 19.XI.1896 MIREK 14.1924-29.VII.1944* EMIL 26.VIII.1877 ELA 29.X.1879 ZDENĚK 15.X.1912-4.VIII.1942* JIŘÍ 3.X.1889 HERMÍNA 11.III.1897-7.RDA 15.IV.1881-23.VI.1942* HELENA 6.III.1936-4.XI.1942* ROBERT 7.VI.1893-26.X.1942* ZDENKA 13.V.1897-6.X.1942* VIKTOR 8.IV.1880-6.X.ZENA 5.IV.1881-23.V.1943* VALFRIE 23.VII.1917-31.VII.1919-8.XI.194* NEU EMIL 6.V.1905 MARTA 25.IV.1913 EVA 24.IV.1937-18.XII.194* BRUNO 25.IX.1895-23.V.1943* EMIL 30.IX.1888 FRIEDA 27.XI.1896 KURT 14.VII.1931-11.III.1943* FRANTIŠEK 19.IV.1897-30.VII.1942* KAREL 2.VIII.1918 ROBERT 3.VII.1917 BERTA 10.XII.1914-16.X.1944* RUDOLF 7.XII.1904-9.III.1942* ANNA 22.VIII.1888 MARKÉTA 4.X.1911-10.VII.1942* HEDVIKA 11.XII.1852-UBRUNN IMRE 23.IV.1897 MARTA 25.VIII.1883-4.XII.1943* TEREZIE 23.VII.1898-12.X.194* NEUBURGOVÁ RŮŽENA 12.X.1884-25.V.1890-9.III.1942* NEUGASSER OTA 7.IV.1897 EDITA 21.X.1894-9.III.1942* RUDOLF 24.VIII.1892-22.X.1942* ERNA 21.1895-4.VIII.194* 5 BEDŘICH 25.VIII.1925-28.IX.194.4* NEUGRÖSCHL BEDŘICH 5.III.1873-15.X.1942* VILÉM 25.XI.1885-4.VIII.1942* HELENA 8.II.1891-16 JIŘÍ 24.X.1922-6.IX.1943* ALEXANDER 31.V.1906 BERTA 27.VIII.1914-12.X.194* ALFRÉD 25.V.1883-12.X.194* ALFRÉD 17.IX.1879-18.V.1944* PA 119.XI.1867 OLGA 15.VIII.1875-26.X.1942* BEDŘICH 5.IV.1890-26.X.1943* BEDŘICH 7.1890-7-? BEDŘICH 22.XII.1893 RŮŽENA 8.V.1900 PAVEL 14.15-13.IX.1942* MARIE 17.VII.1887-6.XII.194.3* EMANUEL 24.II.1877 GUSTA 8.XII.1879 MARIA 3.VII.1916-15.XII.1943* EMANUEL 16.XII.1890 PA 10.VIII.1880-10.VII.1942* ERVIN 16.II.1887 IRMA 7.VI.1895 LUDVÍK 3.V.1924-26.VII.1944* ERVIN 26.VIII.1905-28.XII.1943* FILIP 8.IX.18 9.III.1942* JINDŘICH 12.III.1875 MATYLDA 22.II.1881-26.X.1943* JINDŘICH 27.VIII.1919-30.IV.1942* JINDŘICH 13.V.1925-18.V.1944* JIŘÍ 21.III.II.1927-28.IX.194* JOSEF 7.V.1887-31.VIII.194* JOSEF 20.I.1889-21.X.1941* JOSEF 27.V.1890-6.IX.1943* JOSEF 9.IV.1897-9.I.1942* JOS III.1881-4.VIII.194* LAZAR 22.VII.1875 LEO 25.IV.1895 ELSA 12.V.1903 EVA 26.V.1942* LISELOTA 30.VII.1931-6.IX.1943* LEO 14.V.1897 ADÉLA 13.IX.1900-9.V MORIC 31.XII.1869 ELEONORA 14.XI.1872-17.VII.1942* OSKAR 20.III.1887 ANNA 18.V.1951 KARLA 7.V.1884-14.IX.1942* OSKAR 18.XII.1897* 1897 KLÁRA 6.I.1895 HANA 14.V.1926-6.IX.1943* OTA 13.XII.1903-7* OTA 21.III.1909 REGINA 23.IX.1911-17.VII.1888-31.VII.1942* OSKAR 10.VIII.1897* OR 12.XII.1896 HEDVIKA 1.XII.1909-9.V.1942* VIKTOR 7.1897-13.VII.1944* RUDOLF 18.VI.1886 ŠTĚPÁNKA 31.III.1888-23.I.1943* RUDOLF 19.VIII.95 ALICE 27.VIII.1913-10.VII.1942* ANNA 15.XI.1871-26.X.1943* ANNA 26.IV.1874 RŮŽENA 12.VI.1907 VILÉM 5.XI.1910-18.V.1944* VILÉM 31.VII.1876-15.V.1944* VÍTĚ 3-EMILIE 28.VII.1869-23.VII.1942* JOSEF 26.IV.1893 FRANTIŠKA 7.V.1863-15.V.1944* FRANTIŠKA 20.VII.1884-10.VII.194* FRIEDA 5.IX.1870-22.VII.1942* GAB 36.X.1876-9.V.1942* HELENA 18.II.1899 RUTH 15.IV.1930-18.XII.194* HERMÍNA 16.III.1879* FRANTIŠEK 29.VII.1904-3.XI.1941* HERMÍNA 24.XII.1884 JENY 9.IX.1874-15.V.194* JULIE 28.V.1923-30.IV.194* KAMILA 4.VI.1902-27.X.194* LAURA 23.XI.1879 ELSA 23.VIII.1881 ANNA 8.VIII.1884 P PAVLA 10.VIII.1861-9.V.194* REGINA 11.IX.1866-18.X.1942* REGINA 19.II.1877-28.VII.1942* RŮŽENA 20.VII.1860-7.VII.1942* VALERIE 27.X.1901 JIŘÍ 31.III.1913-18.III.1942* JIŘÍ 22.VII.1911 917-30.XI.194* JOSEF 14.1881 ADÉLA 26.XI.1882-6.X.1943* LEO 6.IV.1908-19.III.1945* PAVLA 30.IX.1907 1897-25.V.194* IDA 3.V.1887-6.IX.1943* MATYLDA 21.VII.1862-19.X.1942* NEUSCHUL ARNOŠT 25.IV.1891 MARTA 14.V.1891* LE ARTUR 28.III.1873 IRENA 31.III.1892-18.XII.1943* HILDA 4.III.1902-13.VII.1942* HILDA 17.VI.1906 HANA 27.X.1933* JEANETTA 31.I.1867-26.X.1942* 76.III.1913* OLGA 14.XI.1877 IRENA 8-9.VI.194* NEUSTEINOVÁ LILY 31.V.1886-25.V.194* NEUWALD GÜNTER 25.XI.1922-9.III.194* NE INA 10.VIII.1877 ERNA 26.VIII.1908 MARGIT 30.VII.1909 VĚRA 30.XII.1930 TOMÁŠ 28.III.1933* MARIA 21.I.III.172.3* MARIE 14.III.1991-26.X.1942* 2.III.1921.1-11.III.194* NISSEL JAKUB 10.III.1879 FRANTIŠKA 8.III.1893-9.V.194* NISSENFELDOVÁ CHAJE MALKA 24.VIII.1868-18.XII.194* NOKOLO PAVEL 1.II ARD 17.VIII.1873-11.V.1944* RUDOLF 14.II.1862-30.VII.1942* EMA 8.II.1877-15.X.1942* OTTILIE 30.III.1111943-5.X.194* NOTHMANNOVÁ VĚRA 21.XII.1907* SKOVÁ VILEMÍNA 17.IV.1892-17.VII.194.3* NOTA EMIL 19.VII.1932-25.VIII.194* NOTHMANNOVÁ VĚRA 21.XII.1907* M.43* JINDŘICH 5.XI.1881 HELENA 13.V.1885 ROBERT 2.II.1922-31.XII.194* JOSEF 1.I.1889-27.VII.1944* KONRAD 14.XII.1894 EMIL 12.V.1942*

The weight of wheels cut the pass ever deeper so that steep walls rose on either side. Here only the bloody rowanberry grew. Ever-heavier wheels kept running over bodies. They stamped bolts of yellow fabric— good, durable fabric—with six-pointed stars. Inside of these stars they printed signs with jagged letters in a foreign language. They ordered all Jews to wear these humiliating signs — signs like for livestock — on the left, just over the heart. Perhaps these marks were put there to quicken the pulse even more, so the heart would grow angular and constrict, or perhaps these were put there only as targets to aim at. And these stars shone even in the light of day.

Robert Kaufman was returning home from the
Bránik quarries to his apartment in Karlín. He was
dead tired from unaccustomed labor and was barely
able to keep on his feet, since he was not allowed
to sit down on the tram. In Podolí a German with
a badge on his lapel boarded the tram. When he saw
the star he grabbed Kaufman by the shoulder, kicked
him, and threw him from the moving tram. Kaufman
fell on the hard stone of the rail-line, lacerating his
face till it bled and breaking a leg. He lay there
for a long time until he was taken to the Jewish
hospital. He was taken there in a wheelbarrow.
On the way Kaufman roused from unconsciousness
and moaned in pain.

REMOVE THY STROKE AWAY FROM ME:
I AM CONSUMED BY THE BLOW OF THINE HAND.
-- Psalms 39:11

Blood was spilled and people were dying by murder or suicide, but these were only streams that had yet to coalesce into that great river of death. And now a hangman appeared who sat in place of the judge. Looking with cruel eyes through the slits of his lids, he began to give orders to hasten the kingdom of death.

On 27 September, 1941, Reinhard Heydrich was named Reichsprotector. When Himmler was recommending him to Hitler, he advised: 'Heydrich knows no mercy, no pity. For him, even the murder of children will be a joyful duty.' Hitler smiled and nodded in agreement. Ordinarily Hitler never smiled. Immediately upon his arrival Heydrich declared martial law, and each day he presided over the deaths of dozens of people. On 16 October the first transport of Jews left for Lodz. On 19 October, Terezín was established as a stop on the way to death. On 11 November, Hitler gave Himmler an order to exterminate the Jews. On 24 November, the first transport of Jews was dispatched to Terezín.

MY TEARS HAVE BEEN MY BREAD
DAY AND NIGHT.
-- Psalms 42:4

People lay about on the cement floor of the exhibition grounds, which consisted of clapboard shacks, the outsides of which had been covered in whitewash that was now smudged with rain blurred soot. Among them were families with children crying, who wanted to go home. A normal day's worth of bathwater had to last a week or longer in the filth and dirt of the wooden shacks. In summer they suffocated in the stench and stifling air, and in winter they shivered with cold. They stuffed their ears with cotton wool to drown out moaning and shrieks. They were also kicked and beaten as their last possessions were taken from them, among them were the most necessary ones. Many people died on the cement floor amid the groaning and squalor. And at night they were then marched under the weight of their luggage onto a train, forced with kicks and scolded in that language of theirs, and packed into cars in order to take them to the place from which there was no return.

Rudolf Kohn was paralyzed and had used a
wheelchair for years. They took him to the
Radiomart in a cart. There he was set on an
ordinary chair. People were called up to a barber
to be cropped short. An SS man was furious when
Kohn did not come when called. They told the SS
that Rudolf Kohn was paralyzed and couldn't walk.
The SS man screamed that he would cure him.
He took out his service revolver and shot it

point-blank at Kohn's ear. Rudolf Kohn jumped up and took a few steps. Then he collapsed and died.

THE VOICE OF HIM THAT TAUNTETH
AND BLASPHEMETH; BY REASON
OF THE ENEMY AND THE REVENGEFUL
-- Psalms 44:17

VIII 1890 MARIE 31.III 1924-6.IX 1943 * FRANTIŠEK 18.VII 1891-16.X 1944 * FRANTIŠEK 23.IV 1900-28.IX 1944 * FRANTIŠEK 21.XII 1902-9.V 1942 * HA
2-6.IX 1943 * JOSEF 17.VII 1903 VLASTA 5.IV 1904-30.IV 1942 * KAREL 11.IX 1878-14.VII 1942 * KAREL 22.X 1881 REGINA 6.IV 1879-17.III 1942 * KAREL
6.IV 1887-? * OTA 19.X 1888 OLGA 2.IV 1887-16.X 1944 * PAVEL 7.VI 1893-20.III 1944 * RICHARD 19.V 1882 BEDŘIŠKA 16.VI 1893-28.X 1944 * RUDOL
* ALOISIE 18.VI 1875-19.X 1942 * ANEŽKA 30.XI 1894 ZLATUŠKA 18.X 1927-8.IX 1942 * ANNA 16.VII 1884-22.X 1942 * ANNA 12.IV 1892-26.X 1942 * AUG
IE 16.IX 1853-26.X 1942 * MARIE 4.VI 1884-22.IV 1942 * MARIE 19.VI 1920-16.X 1944 * MARKÉTA 7.VI 1900-19.X 1944 * MARIA 17.IV 1894-22.IX 1942 * MARIA 12.VI 19
POLATSIK SIMON 26.III 1908 HELENA 9.XII 1913-22.IV 1942 * POLESI DON 11.XII 1901-21.X 1941 * EMIL 16.IV 1907-1.X 1944 LILY 26.VIII 1912-12.X 1944 *
1915-24.I 1945 JINDŘIŠKA 7.XII 1921-1.X 1944 * ALFRÉD 9.IX 1862 MATYLDA 11.VI 1875-19.X 1942 * ANTONÍN 19.II 1874-28.X 1944 * ARNOŠT 6.I 1867 IDA 15.XII 18
901-26.I 1943 * BEDŘICH 8.IX 1902-9.I 1942 * BEDŘICH 11.IX 1911-6.IX 1943 * BEDŘICH 9.IX 1915-15.XII 1943 * BOHDAN 22.IV 1892 RIFKA 2.VI 1884-4.VIII 19
1943 * EVŽEN 24.I 1891-1.X 1944 * EWALD 4.III 1896 OLGA 6.II 1903-6.IX 1943 * FELIX 28.IX 1920-6.IX 1943 * FRANTIŠEK 9.IX 1890 ELA 23.VII 1893-21.X
20.VIII 1900-19.VI 1943 * HANUŠ 4.V 1904 TRUDA 19.XII 1905-6.IX 1943 * HANUŠ 8.XI 1909 ERNA 26.XI 1912-31.X 1941 * HANUŠ 12.XI 1919-15.
III 1865-19.X 1942 ELSA 3.III 1866-28.VIII 1942 * JINDŘICH 24.X 1876-19.X 1942 * JINDŘICH 21.XI 1878 ZDEŇKA 9.XII 1883-27.X 1942 * JINDŘICH 25
6-4.VIII 1942 * JOSEF 28.VII 1882 VALERIE 25.IX 1890-31.X 1941 * JOSEF 7.XII 1883 OLGA 14.IV 1891-9.I 1942 * JOSEF 19.III 1884-14.VII 1943 * JOSEF
US 17.I 1896-1.IV 1942 * JULIUS 25.IV 1896 VĚRA 8.XII 1909-12.VI 1942 * KAMIL 18.X 1876-9.III 1942 * KAREL 18.V 1868-24.VIII 1942 IDA 12.IX 1876-18.V
.IX 1943 OLGA 7.I 1876-18.XII 1943 * LEOPOLD 22.XII 1878 MARIANA 1.III 1894-28.X 1944 EVA 8.III 1923-19.X 1944 * MAX EWALD 3.VII 1875-8.III 1942 *
DA 2.VI 1893-26.V 1942 * OTA 22.X 1882 ARTUR 3.VII 1889-11.III 1942 * OTA 14.IX 1884 HELENA 21.VIII 1896-21.X 1941 * OTA 13.IX 1885 OTILIE 4.IV 18
RICHARD 28.VI 1887 BERTA 10.X 1894 PAVEL 5.VIII 1929-11.III 1942 * ROBERT 14.IV 1885 MARTA 15.IV 1879-22.X 1942 * ROBERT 15.VI 1891 MARIE 2
11.IV 1927-6.IX 1943 * RUDOLF 31.I 1886 GERTRUDA 11.VIII 1902-6.IX 1943 ARNOŠT 30.I 1932-22.VIII 1942 * RUDOLF 9.VI 1889-9.I 1942 * RUDO
1899 HELENA 6.VI 1899 HELGA 11.XII 1928-19.X 1944 * VALTR 18.XI 1913-18.XII 1943 * VALTR 7.V 1921-29.IX 1944 * VIKTOR 14.VI 1883-14.III 1942 *
70-19.X 1942 * ZIKMUND 26.IV 1873-15.V 1944 OLGA 24.V 1880-16.I 1943 * ZIKMUND 13.IX 1873-20.IX 1942 * ADÉLA 9.IV 1883-17.III 1942 * A
1942 * ANNA 24.IX 1878-3.XI 1941 * ANNA 24.IX 1881-23.IV 1942 * ANNA 11.VIII 1885-20.VII 1942 * ANNA 2.XI 1908 KAMILA 17.IV 1944-28.X 194
RTA 28.VI 1867-19.X 1942 * BERTA 31.V 1877-23.IV 1942 * BERTA 25.VIII 1926-4.VIII 1942 * DORA 6.IV 1860-22.VII 1942 * EDITA 18.VIII 1910-20.
NTIŠKA 2.IX 1899-28.X 1944 * GERTRUDA 6.VII 1886-22.X 1942 * GRÉTA 7.VI 1891-15.V 1944 * HANA 6.V 1919-25.IV 1942 * HEDVIKA 4.XI 1877-1.IV 1942 * HEDVIK
1889 GERTRUDA 7.I 1893-20.VIII 1942 * HELENA 30.VIII 1909 MARIE 30.XII 1914-6.IX 1943 * HERMÍNA 4.VI 1868-15.XII 1943 * HERMÍNA 24.XI 1868-3
27.XII 1919-28.IV 1942 * LEONTÝNA 14.VIII 1878-6.IX 1943 * LILY 5.I 1907-25.V 1942 * LILY 1.IV 1927-16.X 1941 * LUISA 10.III 1867-26.X 1942 * MARIANA 30.I 189
9.X 1944 * OLGA ? V 1884 ANNA 7.VI 1915 JOSEF 5.VII 1906-9.I 1942 * OLGA 18.IV 1885-6.IX 1943 * OTILIE 3.V 1886-28.X 1944 * PAVLA 22.I 1897-14.VII 1942 * PAVLÍN
V 1943 * TEREZIE 21.XI 1860-21.X 1942 * VILEMÍNA 31.V 1887-22.X 1942 * VILEMÍNA 25.XII 1897-2.I 1942 EVA 2.III 1924-6.IX 1943 * POLLAK-K
ALŽBĚTA 10.I 1921-20.I 1943 * HERBERT 17.III 1903-3.XI 1941 * MAX 21.VII 1882 MARTA 27.X 1888-25.VIII 1942 * OSVALD 5.VI 1902 VIKTOR 16.VI 19
* JINDŘICH 30.V 1878-3.IX 1944 * KAREL 18.IV 1910-1.X 1944 ZDENKA 11.IX 1912 JANA 18.XII 1941-6.X 1944 * RUDOLF 12.XII 1898 EDITA 14.V 1915-2
3 * OTA 3.III 1900-20.VIII 1942 * NETA 20.XII 1856-31.VII 1942 * OLGA 7.VII 1884-6.IX 1943 * POMERANZ ARNOŠT 10.III 1903-8.III 1945 *
ÉD 7.XII 1886-1.IX 1942 * ANTONÍN 1.X 1894-20.III 1945 * ARNOLD 11.XI 1886-16.III 1942 RUDOLFÍNA 8.XI 1887-28.IV 1942 * ARTUR 7.IV 1902-26.I 1943 *
03-1.X 1944 * EGON 28.III 1908-28.X 1944 * EMIL 31.V 1875-1.VI 1943 * EMIL 1.X 1888-19.III 1942 JULIE 5.V 1890-26.X 1941 * EMIL 4.XI 1891 HELENA 15
IE 18.VI 1894-20.VIII 1942 * FRANTIŠEK 21.VIII 1902 VLASTA 26.IX 1906 INGEBORG 6.VIII 1929 JIŘÍ 19.IV 1936-15.V 1944 * GABRIEL 25.XII 1860-13.I
RÉD 28.III 1942-4.X 1944 * HYNEK 25.VIII 1871 ARNOŠTKA 6.XII 1884-26.X 1942 * JINDŘICH 31.I 1912-7.II 1945 IRMA 12.VIII 1890 ILSA 26.III 1920-
ERMÍNA 10.V 1880-19.X 1942 * JULIUS 11.IX 1895 IRMA 23.X 1898 RALF 1.X 1929-18.V 1944 * KAREL 17.I 1879 JULIE 10.VI 1883-26.X 1942 * KAREL 5.
X 1911-6.IX 1943 * KAREL 28.XI 1917-29.VIII 1943 * LEO 7.V 1908-6.IX 1943 RŮŽENA 16.X 1918-1.X 1944 * LEOPOLD 28.IX 1862 KAMILA 23.X 1873-19.X 19
23.XII 1900 HILDA 14.IX 1906-6.IX 1943 * OTA 26.III 1910-28.IX 1944 * OTA 24.IV 1919-25.XII 1943 * RICHARD 2.VIII 1882 REGINA 30.III 1885-31.X 1941 * RICH
1942 PAVLA 5.II 1883-26.I 1943 * TEODOR 24.XII 1876 IRMA 22.IV 1883-15.XII 1943 * VALTR 14.VII 1913-18.XII 1943 PAVLA 29.VI 1888-28.VII 1942 * VIKTO
15.VIII 1902-21.X 1941 * ZIKMUND 18.X 1863-19.X 1942 ŽOFIE 21.III 1865-26.X 1942 * ZIKMUND 9.III 1880 IRENA 30.XII 1895 LILY 29.V 1922 RITA 8.VIII 19
X 1942 * EMILIE 21.VIII 1869-25.VIII 1942 * EMILIE 19.XI 1870-4.X 1943 * EMILIE 11.III 1882 HELENA 22.VIII 1911-6.IX 1943 * EMILIE 11.VII 1896 STELA 1
1942 * JANA 2.XI 1870-? * JANA 7.X 1878-15.X 1942 * JOSEFA 3.I 1867-19.X 1942 * KAMILA 4.VII 1899 IRENA 2.V 1930 HARY 24.VI 1926-8.X 1942 * KARO
* OLGA 21.VII 1880-8.IX 1942 * PAVLA 26.VIII 1869-22.X 1942 * RŮŽENA 8.I 1880-5.VIII 1942 * RŮŽENA 5.VIII 1881 MARKÉTA 21.VIII 1908-9.I 1942 * RŮ
7.IV 1876-20.VII 1942 RŮŽENA 8.IX 1873-15.X 1942 * ARNOŠT 25.IV 1913 CILI 15.XII 1914-15.I 1942 * ARTUR 7.I 1902 EDITA 5.VII 1916 KAREL
VALTR 16.VII 1900-14.III 1945 * JOSEF 6.VI 1883-9.IX 1943 MARKÉTA 5.XI 1896-15.XII 1943 * JOSEF 20.IV 1888 OTILIE 4.IV 1890 EVA 5.VI 19
924-3.XI 1941 * MAGNUS 16.V 1897 LUDMILA 27.IX 1898-28.X 1944 * MAX 24.V 1877 KAMILA 17.V 1888-6.IX 1943 * MOŘIC 31.VIII 187
29.VI 1885-13.III 1944 * RUDOLF 14.VII 1885 JOSEFA 29.I 1900 HANA 16.I 1923-25.VIII 1942 * RUDOLF 5.VI 1886 IRMA 13.IV 1886-15.I 1942 * R
FRIEDA 1.VIII 1880-23.X 1944 * HEDVIKA 26.VI 1879-4.VIII 1942 * HERMÍNA 25.IV 1874-15.XII 1943 * HERMÍNA 31.I 1875-15.V 1944 * IRMA 7.III 1887-30.VI 1943
30.VII 1905-22.X 1942 * OLGA 16.XI 1884 EDITA 9.II 1919-27.IV 1942 * OTILIE 16.IX 1866-19.X 1942 * PAVLA 6.XII 1879-26.X 1942 * RŮŽENA 20.III 1861
N 12.VII 1895-? * VALTR 12.III 1897-? * POSIN MENDL 15.IX 1870 EMILIE 15.VII 1872-19.X 1942 * RACHEL 5.VIII 1906 NOEMI 1.IV 1932-4.X
44 * KAREL 18.VII 1888 IDA 12.VIII 1902 TOMÁŠ 22.IV 1928-26.I 1943 * OTAKAR 29.VIII 1885-1.IX 1942 * VILÉM 9.VI 1901-29.IX 1944 * VÍTĚZSL
1942 * PREISLEROVÁ ANNA 8.X 1903-8.X 1942 * BERTA 21.IV 1874-21.IV 1944 * MARIE 7.VI 1873-19.X 1942 * PREISS EVŽEN 12.XII 1918-1
RIE 21.X 1892-18.V 1944 * PRESSBURGER HANUŠ 3.III 1896-29.IX 1944 * MAX 23.V 1883 BERTA 18.VI 1882-4.VIII 1942 * RUDOLF 16.II 1869-2
875-19.X 1942 * BERTA 27.III 1889-8.IX 1942 * ELSA 3.III 1886-15.I 1942 * JULIE 16.I 1874-15.XII 1943 * JULIE 16.I 1874-12.XII 1943 * RŮŽENA 9.IX 190
R FRANTIŠEK 26.XII 1904-15.V 1944 * JAROSLAV 17.I 1886-6.IV 1944 * JINDŘICH 18.III 1875 EDWINA 3.IX 1879 OTA 22.IX 1913-21.X 1941 * JIŘÍ 2
5-19.X 1942 * HANA 3.XI 1932-15.V 1944 * JOSEFA 10.III 1899-22.IX 1942 * JULIE 14.VIII 1891-21.X 1941 * MARIE 17.VII 1888 FRANTIŠEK 29.VI 19
1879-22.IX 1942 * PRUSÁKOVÁ REGINA 2.I 1884-17.III 1942 * PRUTHOVÁ EMA 25.V 1879-15.V 1944 * PŘIBORSKÁ ELSA 8.V 1880
1942 * PULTROVÁ KAROLINA 3.III 1876-19.X 1942 * PULZER VIKTOR 2.III 1904-7.II 1945 * PUTZKER EMIL 13.IV 1879 EMILIE 2.I 188
3.XII 1884-9.I 1942 * RABAN MOJŽÍŠ 10.V 1884 RŮŽENA 8.XII 1892-6.IX 1943 * RABER LEOPOLD 4.XII 1908 * GRÉTA 10.VI 1917-27.X
924-21.X 1941 * ZDENĚK 16.VII 1903-28.IX 1944 * KLÁRA 29.IV 1887 MAX 7.I 1931-4.VIII 1942 * MARKÉTA 21.VI 1899-20.VIII 1942 * SELMA 11.V
0-9.X 1944 * RADNITZ FRANTIŠEK 11.XII 1907-14.III 1945 OLGA 25.IX 1879-6.IX 1943 * GUSTAV 28.IV 1876-13.IX 1943 * JULIUS 13.XII 187
A 22.III 1903 HANA RUTH 28.V 1929-6.IX 1943 * BERNARD 14.VII 1848-25.V 1943 * FRANTIŠEK 26.III 1906-24.I 1945 VALERIE 26.VIII 1908-1
X 1943 JANA 18.XII 1865-26.X 1942 * EDITA 25.V 1896-22.IX 1942 VILEMÍNA 26.II 1866-25.X 1942 * RACHMUTH MICHAEL 16.XI 18
896 MARTA 30.V 1900-17.III 1942 * RAMLER JAKUB 28.X 1877 ŽOFIE 14.X 1883-28.VII 1942 * LEO 21.IX 1892-1.IV 1942 * RAND NA
3 * KAREL 30.III 1888 BETY 21.II 1894 CHARLOTA 25.VI 1924 ERIKA 14.II 1926 RUTH 8.XI 1927 GERTA 10.X 1929-11.III 1942 * LEOPOLD 26.II 18
REL 25.IV 1927-8.IX 1942 * IRMA 9.VIII 1888-22.IX 1942 * RATZKAOVÁ OLGA 16.VIII 1890-22.II 1944 * RAUBÍČEK GUSTAV 29.III 1872-22
UDNICKÝ RUDOLF 4.VIII 1890-28.IX 1944 ZDEŇKA 14.V 1897-6.X 1944 HANUŠ 9.VII 1926-28.IX 1944 * RAUDNITZ ALFRÉD 27.IV 1893-
* MARTA 11.VI 1895-15.V 1944 ANNA 7.V 1902-20.III 1944 * OLGA 9.XI 1900-22.IX 1942 * PAVLA 15.VI 1904-9.I 1942 * ROZÁLIE 22.IX 1866-19.
RGER JUDA 10.V 1909-9.III 1945 * RAUSCHER JULIUS 16.III 1876 JULIE 15.XII 1882-25.IV 1942 * RAUSNITZOVÁ REGINA 16.VII 1872-
2 * HEŘMAN 15.VII 1912 NELA 23.II 1917-6.IX 1943 * KURT 4.X 1911-18.XII 1943 * MAXMILIÁN 14.IX 1872-15.XII 1943 * PAVEL 18.III 1881 MARIA
ARTA 17.XI 1878-20.VIII 1942 * RŮŽENA 11.XII 1877 KORNELIE 8.V 1901 MARIE 19.XII 1908-6.IX 1943 * ŠTĚPÁNKA 28.IX 1881-26.X 1942 * REBEC
-8.X 1942 RICHARD 21.X 1896-20.VIII 1942 GERTRUDA 9.X 1905-8.X 1942 * ZIKMUND 3.III 1892 IDA 5.VIII 1895-26.I 1943 * ANNA 25.II 1864-19
1896 GERTA 16.XII 1900 EVA 25.VII 1924-19.X 1944 * KURT 8.IV 1887-14.VII 1942 * MAX 14.I 1897-20.I 1943 * OSKAR 1.V 1889-17.X 1942 OTILIE 1.V 1
OVÁ BETY 12.VII 1902-19.X 1944 * REHOVÁ ARNOŠTKA 11.I 1868-22.X 1942 * RECHENER ARON 26.V 1896-18.V 1944 * RECHNOVSK
937-6.X 1944 * JOSEF 30.V 1889 REGINA 30.X 1887-20.I 1943 * OSKAR 5.III 1903 ŠTĚPÁNKA 14.I 1904-17.V 1942 * MARKÉTA 17.IX 1895-12.X 19
DŘIŠKA 21.X 1894-28.IV 1942 * BERTOLD 23.VIII 1903 FRANTIŠKA 31.VIII 1910 JIŘÍ 22.II 1940-15.XII 1943 * EMIL 11.VI 1881 IDA 21.VIII 1884-
1924-14.III 1945 * JINDŘICH 9.VI 1906-27.II 1945 * JOSEF 5.II 1874 HEDVIKA 11.II 1876-15.X 1942 * JOSEF 21.V 1887 MARKÉTA 14.XI 1899 VĚ
VII 1942 * KAREL 14.V 1921-31.X 1941 * MAX 19.V 1877 OLGA 11.II 1885-6.IX 1943 * MAX 4.IV 1880-21.VII 1942 IRMA 1.VII 1890-6.IX 1943 * M
1875-19.X 1942 * RICHARD 14.VI 1882-17.V 1942 * RUDOLF 2.VIII 1892 ERNA 16.IV 1906 PAVEL 14.XI 1932-6.IX 1943 * RUDOLF 14.XI 1893-7.XII 194
II 1900-15.I 1942 * ELSA 19.II 1899-17.V 1942 * EMILIE 20.XI 1884-15.I 1942 * FRANTIŠKA 30.VIII 1866-24.XII 1942 * GERTRUDA 6.VIII 1901-18.XII 194
UZANA 17.V 1922-6.IX 1943 * REICHEL PAVEL 15.VI 1897-25.IV 1942 * REICHENBACH DAVID 17.II 1888 HEDVIKA 21.IV 1885-27.IV 1942
2 * HANUŠ 9.VI 1906-13.VI 1942 * HEŘMAN 10.VII 1907 ELIŠKA 17.IV 1906 KAREL 12.X 1912 HERTA 24.XII 1920-6.IX 1943 * JAKUB 28.VII 188
1878-26.X 1942 * ANTONÍN 26.IX 1861-23.III 1943 * HERBERT 17.III 1883-11.III 1942 * ROZÁLIE 4.XII 1862-19.X 1942 * TEREZA 16.X 1885-26.X 1942 *
2 * KAREL 10.XII 1893 ANNA 15.XII 1909-18.V 1944 * LEOPOLD 3.V 1932-18.V 1944 * LUDVÍK 22.III 1895-29.IX 1944 * MAXIM 1.XII 1883-26.X 1941
2.X 1895-28.VII 1942 * MARTA 28.III 1890-17.V 1942 * RUTH 10.VII 1934-1.IX 1942 * REICHNER HANUŠ 21.II 1931-4.III 1943 * JINDŘICH 10.
X 1942 * VIKTOR 25.I 1884 HANA 4.II 1891-15.I 1942 * MARIE 10.III 1862-15.X 1942 * REIMANN ALFRÉD 18.VIII 1885-12.X 1944 * EMANUEL 12.
L 13.I 1899 MARKÉTA 4.VIII 1907 EVA 24.V 1935 RUDOLF 24.VIII 1931-26.X 1941 * KAREL 4.I 1907-26.X 1942 VLASTA 18.XII 1911-1.IX 1942
III 1864 OLGA 10.V 1869-19.X 1942 * ANNA 13.I 1884 EDITA 13.X 1907-18.V 1944 * BEDŘIŠKA 15.VI 1871-19.X 1942 * BERTA 17.V 1889-22.IX 1942
2 * REINER ADOLF 15.VIII 1874-7.VIII 1942 ADÉLA 13.XI 1876-26.VII 1942 * ARNOŠT 21.XI 1901-17.V 1942 * EDVARD 15.VII 1905 RŮŽENA
4 PETR 28.IV 1924-18.XII 1943 * JAN 4.IX 1886-? * JOSEF 27.X 1872 SIME 18.III 1874-4.VI 1942 * JULIUS 30.VII 1867 AUGUSTA 24.VI 1876-1
VIKTOR 31.I 1925-17.V 1942 * PETR 12.III 1925-26.I 1943 * ROBERT 19.X 1890 VALERIE 5.IX 1901-6.IX 1943 * ROBERT 24.VII 1907-1.X 1944 * VI
HANA 8.V 1939-18.XII 1943 * MARKÉTA 20.XI 1889-6.IX 1943 * MARTA 22.III 1888-6.IX 1943 * MATYLDA 24.III 1874-19.IX 1942 * PAVLA 9.III 1870
T 9.XII 1899-17.III 1942 * BOHUMIL 5.VII 1907-15.V 1944 * EDVARD 8.II 1904-28.IX 1944 MARTA 12.VII 1907 PETR 31.VIII 1937-6.X 1944 * FILIP 1.V
1910-28.IV 1942 * OSKAR 6.I 1893-28.IX 1944 RŮŽENA 15.I 1889-4.X 1944 JIŘÍ 18.XII 1925-28.IX 1944 * OTA 26.IX 1904-28.X 1944 * OTMAR 14.V
9.X 1942 * OTILIE 15.VII 1876-9.V 1942 * OTILIE 9.III 1909-30.IV 1942 * PAVLA 2.VI 1872-22.X 1942 * RUTH 2.XI 1925-26.X 1942 * RŮŽEN
1879-9.I 1942 * REINITZOVÁ ZDEŇKA 5.X 1891-26.I 1943 * REIS ALFRÉD 23.VIII 1912 RACHIL 10.IX 1909-19.X 1944 * MAX 21.I 1877-1

MILA 26.III 1928-4.X 1944*EMIL 16.X 1895 KLÁRA 19.VIII 1899-11.III 1942*EMIL ? 1898-11.XI 1942*ERVÍN 14.II 1893-17.IV 1942*EVŽEN 25.IV 1891 MARTA 9.X
1943*JAROSLAV 6.X 1879 MARIE 6.V 1890-25.VIII 1942*JAROSLAV 23.X 1888-1.X 1944*JAROSLAV 20.XII 1923-19.X 1944*JINDŘICH 25.VI 1900 CH
2*KAREL 11.XI 1897 BERTA 15.V 1905-13.VI 1942*LADISLAV 11.II 1902-1.X 1944*LUDVÍK 10.VIII 1882-6.IX 1943 ZDEŇKA 25.X 1882-23.VI 1943*L
ÉTA 15.VIII 1899-16.X 1944*RUDOLF 11.VII 1885-30.IV 1942*RUDOLF 24.XI 1894 EMA 19.VI 1906 JOSEF 18.IX 1933 PETR 24.III 1937-28.IV 1942*R
22.IX 1942*BEDŘIŠKA 23.VIII 1897-7.XII 1943*BERTA 31.X 1867-19.X 1942*EMILIE 10.IX 1873-26.X 1942*EMILIE 3.IV 1890-22.IX 1942*GERTRUDA
VIII 1879-4.VIII 1942*REGINA 11.VII 1891-6.IX 1943*RŮŽENA 24.I 1886-14.VII 1942*RŮŽENA 9.VIII 1896-9.X 1942*ZDENKA 20.VIII 1923-16.X 1941*POLAKOF
X 1941*ALBÍNA 3.V 1865-8.XI 1942*FRANTIŠKA 4.IX 1899 EDITA 12.X 1928 KURT 12.X 1928-30.IV 1942*POLINECEROVÁ ILONA 19.I 1907-6.IX 1943*
NOŠT 23.X 1874 HERMÍNA 5.II 1880-15.X 1942*ARNOŠT 6.I 1878 BERTA 23.X 1885-3.XI 1941*ARNOŠT 11.XII 1881 RŮŽENA 21.IV 1888-11.III 1942*ARNOŠT 26
2.IV 1913 EDITA 29.IV 1915-6.IX 1943*EGON 6.II 1894-29.IX 1944*EMIL 21.VIII 1862-20.VII 1942*EMIL 13.II 1875-19.X 1942*EMIL 8.III 1881 EVELINA 24.XII 1894 DO
23.IV 1891 RŮŽENA 19.IX 1891-22.X 1942*FRANTIŠEK 6.II 1894 ANNA 29.XI 1909 IRENA 16.IX 1931-17.III 1942*FRANTIŠEK 18.IX 1896-26.X 1942*F
EDGAR 30.V 1923-6.IX 1943*HANUŠ 24.VI 1923-6.IX 1943*HANUŠ 30.VI 1923-19.XI 1942*HEŘMAN 19.IV 1866-19.X 1942*HEŘMAN 8.I 189
HEDVIKA 6.VI 1891-1.X 1944 LIESELOTA 4.VIII 1921-6.IX 1943 EDITA 19.VI 1932-JIŘÍ 28.II 1939-4.X 1944*JIŘÍ 25.V 1878-27.IV 1942*JIŘÍ 15.II 189
ŠKA 9.XI 1891-19.X 1944 ROBERT K. III 1921-29.IX 1944*JOSEF 21.XI 1888 RŮŽENA 20.I 1887-16.X 1944 HANA 21.V 1919-23.X 1944*JOSEF 29.VI 1891
1881 ANNA 8.VIII 1885-20.VIII 1942*KAREL 6.II 1895-29.IX 1944 HILDA 31.V 1901-4.X 1944*KAREL 26.XII 1898-13.II 1943*KAREL 15.VIII 1903-9
LSA 15.II 1878-17.III 1942*MAX 4.XII 1915-1.X 1944*MOŘIC 1.VIII 1870-19.X 1942*MOŘIC 4.I 1879 EMILIE 15.VII 1881-18.XII 1943 KAREL 9.XI 1922-28.
A 28.VI 1887 HILDA 26.X 1904 MARKÉTA 3.XII 1928-11.III 1942*OTA 29.IX 1891-11.III 1942*OTA 14.III 1892-9.I 1942*OTA 19.V 1894 MARIE 20.V 1899
5.I 1933-15.XII 1943*RUDOLF 21.V 1874 FRANTIŠKA 13.II 1874-19.X 1942*RUDOLF 21.I 1876 LUISA 8.XI 1887-6.IX 1943*RUDOLF 4.II 1883 ANNA 21.
42 GERTRUDA 5.V 1897-9.V 1942*RUDOLF 8.IV 1892 HEDVIKA 1.I 1900-16.X 1944*RUDOLF 18.V 1895 LILY 10.I 1902-16.X 1944*RUDOLF 2.VII
O EMILIE 27.V 1880 KLÁRA 31.III 1886-17.III 1942*VILÉM 21.I 1860-15.X 1942 ŽOFIE 10.V 1865-27.III 1944*VILÉM 20.IV 1885-11.X 1941*VILÉ
EDŘICH 29.X 1915-26.X 1943*ALBÍNA 14.XII 1872-28.III 1943*ALICE 14.IX 1880-17.III 1942*ALICE 22.XI 1901-8.X 1942*ALICE 20.X 1907-21.X
VIII 1862-19.X 1942*ARNOŠTKA 17.II 1866-19.X 1942*ARNOŠTKA 3.V 1868-22.X 1942*ARNOŠTKA 5.V 1893-9.I 1942*ARNOŠTKA 20.XI 18
913-22.X 1942*ELSA 29.V 1882-4.VIII 1942*ELSA 23.VIII 1882-24.XII 1942*ELSA 5.I 1885-30.IV 1942*ELSA 1.V 1900-16.X 1941*EMA 28.II 188
NA 9.VIII 1890-4.VIII 1942*HEDVIKA 19.II 1884-28.IV 1942*HEDVIKA 28.I 1885-26.X 1942*HEDVIKA 24.V 1887-6.IX 1943*HEDVIKA 15.VI 1895 ALEXANDRA
MÍNA 6.VII 1877-27.IV 1942*HILDA 1.IV 1897-20.VIII 1942*IDA 17.VII 1871-22.X 1942*IDA 20.XII 1885-12.X 1944*IRENA 10.III 1882-28.IV 1942*IRMA 6.VIII
V 1904-13.VI 1942*MARIE 30.VIII 1901-20.VIII 1942*MARIE 18.VIII 1921 HANA 3.VIII 1920-6.IX 1943*MARKÉTA 21.II 1890-25.VIII 1942*MARKÉTA 20.II 1895-25
*REGINA 28.XI 1855-23.VIII 1943*REGINA 8.V 1877-12.X 1942*REGINA 6.VIII 1877-15.XII 1943*REGINA 25.X 1890-10.VI 1942*RŮŽENA 21.III 1847-22.IX 1942*RŮŽ
VILLIBALD 28.II 1895-9.I 1942*POLLAK-STERN HANUŠ 20.XI 1899 EDITA 11.V 1901-11.III 1942*POLLAKOVÁ-STRÁNSKÁ IDA 1.IV 18
DOLF 11.V 1898-9.I 1942*AMÁLIE 2.XI 1882-9.I 1942*ELIŠKA 14.IV 1880-4.IV 1943*HELENA 7.IX 1871-23.XII 1942*JINDŘIŠKA 26.II 1870-19.X
7.V 1899-22.VII 1944*POLLITZER EMIL 25.IX 1886-21.X 1941 HELENA 10.II 1902-1.III 1942*JOSEF 7.VII 1912-20.VIII 1942*HERTA 15.III 1924-25
1942*POPEL OTA 25.I 1889 ERNA 29.VII 1900-16.X 1944*POPELÍK JOSEF 11.VII 1893-4.VIII 1942*EMILIE 15.XII 1872-19.X 1942*POPOV
HEDVIKA 16.VIII 1893-18.V 1944*BEDŘICH 20.XII 1888-16.IX 1942*BEDŘICH 4.IV 1899-12.III 1942*BEDŘICH 15.X 1899 PAVLA 12.XII 1905 EVA IVON
1933-18.XII 1943*EMIL 10.II 1901 MARIE 8.III 1892-9.I 1942*EMIL 9.VI 1905-31.X 1941*ENRICO 12.VIII 1860-23.VII 1942*ERVÍN 24.X 1890 ARN
VI 1879 OLGA 23.VIII 1888-8.IX 1942*GABRIEL 12.IV 1880-25.VIII 1942*GUSTAV 3.III 1870 LUDMILA 5.V 1876-19.X 1942*HANUŠ 1.VII 1902 HELENA 13
VIII 1878 EMILIE 28.V 1891-26.X 1942*JIŘÍ 31.VIII 1878 EMILIE 28.V 1891-26.X 1942*JIŘÍ 16.V 1890-26.II 1943 MARIE 20.III 1895-6.IX 1943*JIŘ
LEONTINA 3.XI 1891-7.II 1943 LORA 2.XI 1921-4.I 1942*KAREL 24.XII 1889 KAMILA 18.V 1890 JIŘÍ 22.VIII 1926-8.IX 1942*KAREL 19.VIII 1891-20.VIII
1872-19.X 1942*LUDVÍK 24.III 1878-14.VIII 1942*LUDVÍK 9.X 1893-10.VI 1942*MARKUS 27.IX 1870-27.IX 1942*MAX 26.IV 1889 MARKÉTA 13.XII 1894-2
1944 IDA 12.I 1888-4.X 1944*LEO 16.X 1905-23.IV 1945*RICHARD 12.II 1890-4.VIII 1942*RUDOLF 23.IV 1880-4.VIII 1942*RUDOLF 8.III 1886-9.I 1942*RU
II 1888-1.X 1942*VIKTOR 30.VI 1898-28.X 1944*VILÉM 29.XI 1883 IRMA 21.X 1942 EVA 22.III 1923-16.X 1944*VILÉM 7.III 1889-28.X 1944*VILÉM 6.
BĚTA 29.III 1860-19.X 1942*AMÁLIE 27.II 1868-19.X 1942*ANDĚLA 1.III 1869-28.XII 1942*AUGUSTA 26.IX 1864-29.XII 1942*AUGUSTA 4.X 1890 MARI
*FRANTIŠKA 2.VI 1886 MARKÉTA 12.IX 1920-6.IX 1943*FRANTIŠKA 5.XII 1906-12.X 1944*FRIDA 5.VIII 1880-4.VIII 1942*HEDVIKA 7.XI 1874-15.V 19
1942*KLÁRA 21.IX 1875-19.X 1942*LUISA 7.IV 1870-19.X 1942*MALVÍNA 1.XII 1877-18.VIII 1942*MALVÍNA 9.VII 1886-6.IX 1943*MARIE 6.II 1890-11.III 1942*M
X 1941*VALERIE 13.X 1904-1.IV 1942*VĚRA 16.X 1921-18.V 1944*POPPOVÁ FRANTIŠKA 15.XII 1899-10.II 1943*POR MAXMILIÁN 19.XI 1878
43*BOHUMIL 22.XII 1857-19.X 1942*BOHUMIL 9.VI 1904-26.X 1942*EMANUEL 20.XII 1900-14.IX 1943*FRANTIŠEK 15.I 1904-18.V 19
JOSEF 26.XI 1900-20.IV 1945 MILADA 27.XII 1909 RONALD 11.V 1934-6.X 1944*JOSEF 4.VII 1901 HANUŠ 31.VIII 1932-16.X 1944*KAREL 21.X
CA 24.VIII 1886-19.X 1944*OSKAR 31.VII 1901-24.I 1945*OTA 8.IV 1888 ELIŠKA 15.X 1896 PAVEL 29.VI 1921 ARNOŠT 17.XI 1925-6.IX 1943*O
3-28.IX 1944*RUDOLF 23.XI 1910-28.VIII 1942*RUDOLF 24.III 1916 VĚRA 29.XI 1918-6.IX 1943*VALTR 27.V 1901-15.XII 1943*VIKTOR 1.V 18
19.VII 1944*JOSEFA 3.V 1876-19.X 1942*JULIE 22.II 1859-19.X 1942*JULIE 22.III 1877-15.X 1942*KLÁRA 5.II 1897 LUDMILA 2.VII 1922-4.VIII 1942*MALVÍNA 7.
A 23.VI 1899-4.X 1944*PORIAS ADOLF 9.VII 1867-15.VIII 1942*EDVARD 1.XI 1894-28.IX 1944*LEO 29.X 1893-31.III 1942*PORTHEIM BED
14 REGINA 15.IV 1906-8.X 1942*POSNEROVÁ ANNA 24.X 1877-18.XII 1943*POSTOLKOVÁ IRMA 9.X 1914-14.XII 1942*POTM
ELA 22.IX 1884-4.VIII 1942*HELENA 1.V 1881-16.X 1944*LUDMILA 11.XI 1867-15.IX 1942*MARIE 23.XII 1870-15.X 1942*PRÁGROVÁ BOŽ
XII 1907 ETEL 9.XI 1877-26.I 1943*LUCIE 12.I 1914-11.III 1942*PREISSLER FRANTIŠEK 24.II 1902-26.II 1942*KAREL 25.VI 1897-6.IX 1943*OTA
1883-26.XII 1942*KLÁRA 18.IV 1897-27.IV 1942*PRESSER ERVÍN 26.VII 1915-23.IV 1944*JAKUB 28.XII 1862-23.X 1942*KAREL 29.XI 1917-25
NZ HERBERT 18.XI 1896-29.IX 1944*JOSEF 3.VII 1875 HEDVIKA 17.I 1878-22.X 1942*PRISANT ALEXANDR 7.X 1891-9.I 1942*PRISKEROV
NA 13.V 1894 HANA 11.VI 1921-15.I 1942*JOSEF 1.VIII 1926-6.IX 1943*KAREL 8.XI 1890-1.X 1944 DORA 12.III 1897-28.X 1944*PAVEL 18.VIII 1914 M
ENA 4.VIII 1894-6.IX 1943*PROSKAUER JINDŘICH JOSEF 30.VII 1904 RITA 23.X 1904-9.I 1942*OSKAR 3.VIII 1879 JANA 26.VII 1920-15.XI
BRAM HUGO 4.I 1881-19.V 1943*ROBERT 22.VII 1880-4.VIII 1942*PŘÍHODOVÁ ELA 20.IX 1903-29.III 1943*PTÁČEK JAN 18.VI 1889-
AN 4.VIII 1874-30.IV 1943 ŽOFIE 16.XI 1881-9.X 1944*RUDOLF 22.VI 1892-20.XII 1943*FRANTIŠKA 25.VI 1875-19.X 1942*PYROVÁ OLGA 10
K EMIL 17.IV 1878 JOSEFA 16.IV 1882-8.IX 1942*RABINOVITZ MOŘIC 28.X 1896 MATYLDA 7.VI 1905 SIEGBERT 20.VII 1926-15.IX
*RÁBL EMIL 24.VIII 1883 RŮŽENA 12.V 1891-23.X 1944 JULIUS 14.VII 1872 FRANTIŠKA 1.XII 1874-19.X 1942*MAX 15.X 1882 RŮŽENA
AKAR 31.XII 1883 ERNA 24.VI 1892-4.VIII 1942*MARTA 23.X 1868-11.III 1942*RADNITZER KAREL 29.VIII 1912-17.IV 1943*HANA 22.II
XI 1866-26.IV 1943 KAMILA 26.VIII 1877-15.XII 1943*RADOVICIOVÁ LILY 19.II 1903-4.VIII 1942 ADÉLA 16.VIII 1878-28.VII 1943*RA
8-15.XII 1943*RAICHARTOVÁ JOSEFA 26.X 1916-?*RAIK ROBERT 28.VIII 1902-24.III 1945*RAIMANN VÍTĚZSLAV 25.IX 1
4.VII 1944*GUSTA 14.V 1892-15.V 1944 SAMUEL 7.VIII 1923-6.IX 1943*RANDA HEŘMAN 16.I 1878 GERTRUDA 29.VI 1893-25.VIII 194
1897-26.X 1942*MAX 8.III 1884-28.X 1944 LOTKA 6.IV 1886-20.I 1944*IRENA 11.I 1920-15.I 1942*LILY 20.V 1892-4.VIII 1942*RATH HYN
TSCHEK ALFRÉD 13.XI 1895 ZDEŇKA 18.V 1897-6.IX 1943 JOSEF 8.VI 1922-20.VIII 1942*OTAKAR 27.I 1892-11.III 1942*VALTR 28.VIII 1914-2
NA 25.IX 1896-20.V 1944 PETR 6.VII 1934 HANA 20.VI 1928-21.X 1941 GUSTAV 29.V 1900-22.III 1942*ARNOLD 21.VIII 1886-9.I 1942*ARNOŠT 2
29.XI 1899 JAN MICHAEL 23.II 1930-21.X 1941*RAUCH DAVID 20.XII 1897 BOŽENA 26.VI 1900 RENÉE 12.VIII 1929-6.IX 1943*ELIŠKA
ITZ JULIUS 1.IV 1880 ADÉLA 11.I 1900-20.VIII 1942*RAYNALOVÁ RŮŽENA 11.XII 1871-10.VIII 1942*REACH ALOIS 4.I 1889-1.X 1944 MA
NALIESA 1.III 1922-22.X 1942*PAVEL 2.IX 1906-28.III 1945 VĚRA 6.XII 1919 GITA 3.X 1941 MICHAL 6.II 1944-23.X 1944*RUDOLF 2.XII 1879 KAMILA
.V 1879-22.X 1942*REBENWURZEL ARNOŠT 20.V 1912-6.IX 1943*FRANTIŠEK 1.V 1906-28.IX 1944 KLÁRA 25.VIII 1904-6.X 1944*OTA 24.VI
1.IX 1898-15.I 1942*KAMILA 14.X 1874-15.X 1942*KAROLÍNA 31.X 1908-22.X 1942*REGINA 17.I 1879-4.VIII 1942*REDISCH ARNOŠT 3.II
TA 10.VIII 1882-22.II 1943*ILSA 3.VI 1912 EDITA 31.V 1934-17.V 1942*IRMA 4.X 1891-18.XII 1943*JANA 1.VIII 1876-19.X 1942*REDLINGER M
77-19.X 1942*RECHT ALFRÉD 29.XII 1912 MARTA 18.II 1911-30.IV 1942*LEO 6.IV 1938-16.II 1943*RICHARD 27.V 1875-4.III 1944*VILÉM 18.
OPOLD 26.IX 1892 RACE 12.XII 1891 JIŘÍ 4.I 1926 LEO 28.IV 1929-17.V 1942*REICH ADOLF 17.IV 1902 HERMA 27.XII 1911 ALŽBĚTA 9.IV 1938-1
8.VIII 1887-21.XII 1943*ERICH 11.VI 1911-15.XII 1943 PAVEL 13.I 1939-15.IX 1942*GUSTAV 24.XII 1894 MILADA 3.VIII 1909 JAN 20.V 1937-25.V 194
BĚTA 19.I 1926-17.V 1942*JOSEF 26.I 1910 PETR 9.IV 1938-15.XII 1943*JULIUS 8.V 1869 MALVÍNA 18.XII 1880 OTA 7.III 1914-26.X 1942*KARL
-31.VII 1942 ELSA 12.III 1886-4.X 1944*NATHAN 22.II 1877 BERTA 1.X 1880-27.IV 1942*OSKAR 18.XII 1876 IRMA 22.VI 1885-15.XII 1943*O
97 VALERIE 31.I 1905-9.I 1942*VALTR 28.X 1891 OLGA 25.IV 1891 ZUZANA 23.X 1929-15.VIII 1942*VALTR 16.V 1911-5.X 1943*VILÉM 9.XII 1891 MA
1882-26.X 1942*HELENA 19.VIII 1881-17.V 1942*IRMA 14.II 1886 PAVLA 1.V 1890-20.VIII 1942*KAMILA 14.XII 1885-27.V 1942*LAURA 16.VI 1886-
AUM ARTUR 17.XI 1896-31.XII 1944*HUGO 3.IV 1902 LUISA 8.I 1910-17.V 1942*GRÉTA 16.V 1909-22.IX 1942*RŮŽENA 25.III 1871-15.XI
1893-8.IX 1942*KURT 23.V 1911 MARIANA 14.IX 1917-6.IX 1943*LEOPOLD 24.XII 1870-19.X 1942*MAX 15.I 1884 HILDA 16.VII 1895-6.IX 1943 J
PETR 15.V 1922-18.XII 1943*VILIAM 3.X 1900-6.IX 1943 OLGA 16.III 1867-12.IX 1942*REICHMANN ALFRÉD 16.IX 1875-12.VIII 1942*A
21.VI 1897-28.IX 1944 IRMA 31.XII 1894-9.X 1944*MOŘIC 3.XII 1897-19.X 1944*OTA 13.V 1882 LOTA 1.IX 1878-25.V 1942*OTA 29.IV 1898-2
R 2.IX 1906-15.XII 1943*JOSEFA 26.XI 1860-3.III 1944*KAMILA 28.VII 1875-14.VII 1942*RŮŽENA 24.I 1874-19.X 1942*REICHSFELDO
MIL 23.XII 1896 FRANTIŠKA 10.III 1906-17.V 1942*FRANTIŠEK 16.IX 1890 ANNA 9.III 1894-26.I 1943*FRANTIŠEK 15.IX 1910 MARIE 30.XI
IV 1920-26.X 1942*KAREL 1.IV 1912-9.I 1942*LEOPOLD 28.I 1865-1.I 1942 OTILIE 5.IX 1875-6.X 1944*OSVALD 14.III 1884-16.X 194
2.V 1942*HERMÍNA 29.XI 1873-5.IX 1942*IDA 2.V 1878-22.X 1942*MARTA 9.III 1882-26.X 1942*REIMEROVÁ MARIE 17.XII 1902-?
43*ERICH 23.IX 1904-19.II 1943*ERVÍN 14.II 1904-15.XII 1943*FELIX 25.X 1880-13.VII 1942 FRANTIŠKA 11.X 1885-6.IX 1943*HUGO 21.
3.I 1897-?*KAREL 1.XI 1916-6.IX 1943*KURT 25.VI 1929-16.X 1944*LADISLAV 6.V 1883 HERMÍNA 16.XII 1883 MIROSLAV 4.V 1928-15.I
7.III 1942*VÍTĚZSLAV 1.X 1879 MATYLDA 25.VIII 1877-17.V 1942*ALICE 2.XII 1920-6.XI 1942*ANNA 26.VIII 1902 MARIE 19.V 1899-15.I 1942*
NHALTOVÁ ELSA 18.VII 1892-17.V 1942*REINHARD HUGO 24.XI 1913-16.II 1943*REINHART ALEXANDR 1.V 1895-29.IX 1944*REI
I 1909-15.XII 1943 EVA 11.III 1940-20.II 1943*HUGO 8.III 1881 RŮŽENA 11.VI 1881-12.III 1942*JAROSLAV 26.V 1892-28.IX 1944 EMA 31.VII 189
DA 12.X 1885-6.IX 1943*RUDOLF 1.XI 1880 ELIŠKA 10.II 1887-15.I 1942*RUDOLF 31.X 1909-15.XII 1943*VALTR 14.VIII 1913-19.XII 1944*ADO
1942*REINISCHOVÁ-LÖWYOVÁ GERTRUDA 2.VIII 1902-18.XII 1943*REINIS EMIL 30.VIII 1888 ELSA 1.X 1899 PAVEL 30.
A 6.VII 1880-9.V 1942*VILÉM ? 1916-6.IX 1943*VIKTOR 1.VII 1875-2.VI 1943 KLÁRA 6.II 1881-6.IX 1943*ELSA 10.XII 1882-17.V 1942*HERM

They went slowly, packed into train cars—men, women and children. They went in early spring when the earth smells fresh, they went past streams and rivers, fields and meadows, past well-dressed people running off to have fun or to meet a sweetheart, past people leaning against ploughs, past factories where people stood at lathes watching each turn with care, past puppets shows and past pubs with chinking glasses and the smell of roasting meat, past stores displaying hats, and past moving vans carrying furniture to new apartments, past trains laden with missiles, and past soldiers on motorcycles with pistols in their belts. However they saw nothing, as the windows had been boarded up. And this is how they were cast out on the long journey to a small country station.

Růžena Hekšová had a lot of luggage as well as
a heavy bag filled with provisions. She had been
told that there wasn't much food at Terezín. She
also had suitcases with linens and clothing. Her
transport number was written in white on her
suitcases. A young man with an armband came
by and offered to assist her. Růžena Hekšová was
pleased by his willingness to help. She never saw
her suitcases or bags again. But sometime later she
did see her thermos in a junk shop. She recognized
it immediately because it was painted three different

colours, a gift from abroad. The thermos was for sale, but Hekšová could not buy it because she had no Terezín money.

TRUST NOT IN OPPRESSION,
AND PUT NOT VAIN HOPE IN ROBBERY;
IF RICHES INCREASE, SET NOT YOUR
HEART THEREON
-- Psalms 62:11

They drove them into barracks and forced them to sleep in attics on hard three-tiered bunks. They gave each person three unpeeled, frostbitten potatoes or some slops that at one time they had called coffee, and another time, soup. Even this refuse had to be earned with hard labour. Behind the ramparts trees blossomed, the highway spread into the distance, and beyond the fortress rose green hills. But the city was full of filth and dust, and the clamour of footsteps resounded all day until all were ordered back to their communal quarters.

Adolf Horovic was seventy. He stood in line at the
cafeteria, waiting patiently for two hours. The
cook poured a ladle of brown liquid into his bowl.
Weakened from the wait, he stumbled and fell. The
soup slopped out of the bowl and spilled on the dirt
floor. Horovic did not get a second helping of soup.
He wasn't entitled to one. He sat on the ground and
tears streamed from his eyes. That was all he had for
dinner.

THEY PUT POISON IN MY FOOD,
AND IN MY THIRST THEY GAVE ME VINEGAR
TO DRINK
-- Psalms 69:22

Corpses were carried away in funeral carts that had once been used to deliver bread. There were a lot of corpses, and people paid no attention to the crates in which they were laid. And dust settled over the city and into people's noses as they plodded along, sneezing. They lay in their quarters and talked about their former lives, lives that were beautiful and full of good food. Back then they traveled by train and automobile on trips to tourist inns where music played. And when they came home, they had drawn hot steaming baths and soaked long and blissfully until it was time to dry off with a towel, put on a dressing gown and pajamas before lying down on white, clean-smelling sheets. Then they would settle down for a while with a good book, turn the knob on the radio to hear what was happening in the world. Then sleep would come.

All the blind people were billeted together as they waited for death. For them – and only them – it would be a kind of redemption. They did not see what was going on, yet they knew. The lunatics—fools that had already left this world for another one—were kept in the same barracks. They had already left this world for another, one where they were not given orders. But even the lunatics knew. Then came the handicapped, those missing arms or legs. They were the worst off, because they saw and they knew what was happening.

CONSIDER, YE THE BRUTISH AMONG THE PEOPLE AND YE FOOLS, WHEN WILL YE UNDERSTAND?
-- Psalms 94:8

JARMILA 16.III 1928-4.X 1942 * EMIL 16.X 1895 KLARA 11.IX 1899-11.III 1942 * EMIL 2.1898-11.XI 1942 * ERVÍN 18.I 1896-12.IV 1942 * ERVEN 25.IV 1891 KLARA
2-6.IX 1942 * JAROSLAV 6.X 1879 MARIE 6.V 1890-25.VIII 1942 * JAROSLAV 23.X 1888 1.X 1942 * JAROSLAV 20.XII 1923-19.XII 1943 * JINDŘICH 25.VIII 1890
.0.IV 1942 * KAREL 11.XI 1897 BERTA 15.V 1905 13.V 1942 * LADISLAV 11.X 1902-1.X 1942 * LUDVÍK 10.VIII 1882-6.IX 1943 ZDEŇKA 25.X 1882-23.XII 1942
MARKÉTA 15.VIII 1899-16.XII 1942 * RUDOLF 11.VIII 1885-30.IV 1942 * RUDOLF 24.X 1889 EMA 19.V 1 1906 JOSEF 18.IX 1933 PETR 24.XII 1937-28.IV 1942
1880-22.IX 1942 * BEDŘIŠKA 23.III 1884 BERTA 16.X 1867-19.X 1942 * EMILIE 10.X 1873-26.X 1942 * EMIL 6.I 1890-22.X 1942 * GER
OLGA 6.XII 1879-4.VIII 1942 * REGINA 11.VII 1891-6.X 1942 * RŮŽENA 26.X 1886 14.VII 1942 * RŮŽENA 2.VIII 1896-9.X 1942 * POLA
1894-31.X 1942 * ALBÍNA 5.V 1865-8.X 1942 * FRANTIŠKA 4.IX 1899 EDITA 12.X 1928 KURT 12.X 1928-30.IV 1942 * POLÍNE CEROVÁ ILONA 11.1907-6.X 1942
.* ARNOŠT 23.X 1884 HERMÍNA 15.II 1880-15.X 1942 * ARNOŠT 6.I 1878 BERTA 23.X 1885-3.XII 1942 * ARNOŠT 11.XII 1881 RŮŽENA 21.IV 1888-11.XII 1942 * ARN
SLAV 12.IV 1942 EDITA 29.IV 1915-6.XII 1943 * EGON 6.II 1894-29.XI 1942 * EMIL 21.VIII 1862-20.VII 1942 * EMIL 25.VII 1892 19.X 1942 * EMIL 8.VIII 1880 EVELINA 24.XII 1
ŠEK 6.III 1891 RŮŽENA 19.IX 1891-27.IX 1942 * FRANTIŠEK 6.III 1894 ANNA 29.XI 1909 IRENA 15.I 1931-11.III 1942 * FRANTIŠEK 18.IX 1896-26.X 1942
HANUŠ EDGAR 30.IV 1923-6.X 1943 * HANUŠ 21.VII 1923-6.III 1943 * HANUŠ 25.III 1925 19.XI 1942 * HERMAN 19.IV 1866 19.X 1942 * HERMAN
.0.IV 1944 HEDVIKA 16.V 1891-1.IX 1942 LIESELOTA 14.IX 1921-29.IX 1942 3 EDITA 19.VIII 1942 * JIŘÍ 28.III 1939-4.IX 1944 * JIŘÍ 25.IV 1878-22.IV 1942 * JIŘÍ
ŠEDŘIŠKA 9.XI 1891-19.XI 1942 * ROBERT IV 1887-1.IX 1891-29.X 1942 * JOSEF 21.VIII 1888 RŮŽENA 20.I 1887-16.X 1942 * HANA 2.IV 1919-23.X 1942 * JOSEF 29.V
EL 2.VIII 1881 ANNA 8.VIII 1885-20.VIII 1942 * KAREL 6.II 1895-29.IX 1942 * HILDA 3.IV 1901-4.X 1942 * KAREL 26.XI 1898-13.III 1943 * KAREL 15.VIII 1897
AM ELSA 15.II 1878-11.VII 1942 * MAX 4.XII 1915-1.X 1942 * MOŘIC 5.VII 1870-8.X 1942 * MOŘIC 4.I 1879 EMILIE 15.VIII 1881-18.X 1942 3 KAREL 9.XI 1892
.2 OTA 23.IV 1887 HILDA 26.X 1902 MARKÉTA 3.X 1898-11.III 1942 * OTA 29.X 1891-11.III 1942 * OTA 14.VIII 1871-27.X 1942 * OTA 19.V 1894 MARIE 20.I
ETR 15.III 1933-15.V 1942 * RUDOLF 21.VII 1874 FRANTIŠKA 13.III 1874-19.X 1942 * RUDOLF 21.XI 1876 LUISA 8.XI 1887-6.XII 1942 3 RUDOLF 4.II 1883 AD
.0-9.VII 1942 GERTRUDA 31.VIII 1897-9.V 1942 * RUDOLF 8.IV 1892 HEDVIKA 11.I 1900-16.X 1942 * RUDOLF 18.V 1895 LILY 13.V 1900-16.X 1942 * RUDO
.6.II 1890 EMÍLIE 27.V 1880 BLAŽA 31.III 1886-19.X 1942 * VILÉM 21.I 1860-15.X 1942 2 OFIE 10.V 1865-27.III 1942 * VILÉM 20.IV 1885-11.X 1942
1896 BEDŘICH 29.X 1915-26.X 1942 * ALBÍNA 14.XII 1877-28.III 1942 3 ALICE 1.X 1880-17.III 1942 * ALICE 22.XII 1901-8.X 1942 * ALICE 20.1
TKA 11.VIII 1862-19.X 1942 * ARNOŠTKA 11.XII 1866-19.X 1942 * ARNOŠTA 3.V 1868-22.X 1942 * ARNOŠTKA 5.X 1893-9.III 1942 * ARNOŠT 2.0.I
E 31.I 1913-22.X 1942 * ELSA 29.V 1882-4.VIII 1942 * ELSA 23.VIII 1882-24.XII 1942 * ELSA 5.I 1885-30.IV 1942 * ELSA 1.V 1900-16.X 1943 * EMMA 28
RŮŽENA 2.VIII 1890-4.VIII 1942 * HEDVIKA 11.I 1884-26.X 1942 HEDVIKA 21.III 1885-26.X 1942 * HEDVIKA 16.IV 1887-6.IX 1943 * HEDVIKA 31.III 1895 ALEXA
* HERMÍNA 6.VII 1877-27.IV 1942 * HILDA 1.IV 1897-20.VIII 1942 * IDA 17.VI 1871-22.X 1942 * IDA 10.XII 1885-12.X 1944 * IRENA 10.III 1882-28.IV 1942 * IRMA
IANA 3.V 1904-15.VII 1942 * MARIE 30.VII 1901-20.VIII 1942 * MARIE 18.XII 1921 HANA 3.VII 1925-19.X 1942 * MARKÉTA 21.II 1878-23.VIII 1942 * MARKÉTA 20.III
.CH WILLI BAL D 28.II 1895-19.X 1942 * POLLAK-STERN HANUŠ 20.XI 1899 EDITA 11.V 1901-11.III 1942 * POLLÁKOVÁ-STRÁNSKÁ 21
3 RUDOLF 31.III 1898-9.III 1942 * AMÁLIE 23.XI 1882-9.III 1942 * ELIŠKA 17.V 1880-4.IV 1943 * HELENA 7.IX 1871-23.XII 1942 * JINDŘIŠKA 26.II 1870
ANITA 7.V 1899-22.IX 1942 3 POLLITZER EMIL 25.IX 1886 21.X 1943 HELENA 20.II 1900-12.XII 1942 * JOSEF 7.VII 1912-20.VIII 1942 * HERTA 15.III
.78-17.VI 1942 3 POPEL OTA 25.II 1889 ERNA 29.VII 1900-16.X 1942 * POPELÍK JOSEF 11.VI 1893-4.VIII 1942 * EMILIE 15.XII 1872-19.X 1942 * PO
.0.XI 1884 HEDVIKA 16.VIII 1893-18.V 1944 * BEDŘICH 24.III 1901 IRMA 16.XII 1942 * BEDŘICH 4.V 1899-12.III 1943 * BEDŘICH 5.1899 PAVEL 12.XII 1905 EV
IN 24.III 1933-18.X 1942 * EMIL 10.II 1901 MARIE 8.III 1892-9.III 1942 * EMIL 9.VII 1905-31.X 1942 * ENRICO 12.VII 1860-23.VIII 1942 * ERVÍN 24.X 1890
.RIEL 6.VIII 1879 OLGA 23.IX 1888-8.X 1942 * GABRIEL 12.IV 1880-25.VIII 1942 * GUSTAV 3.III 1870 LUDMILA 6.V 1876-19.X 1942 * HANUŠ 7.VII 1902-HEI
JIŘÍ 31.VIII 1878 EMILIE 7.8.V 1891-6.X 1942 * JIŘÍ 31.VIII 1878 EMILIE 7.8.V 1891-16.X 1942 * JIŘÍ 16.V 1890-26.II 1942 * MARIE 20.III 1895-6.IX 1943 * KA
V 1943 LEONTINA 3.XI 1891-21.IV 1942 LORA 2.XI 1921-4.III 1942 * KAREL 24.XI 1889 KAMILA 18.V 1890-19.X 1942 * JIŘÍ 27.VII 1926-8.XII 1943 * KAREL 12.VII 1891
KLO.X 1882-19.X 1942 * LUDVÍK 24.II 1878-14.VII 1942 * LUDVÍK 6.V 1893-10.V 1942 * MARKUS 27.X 1870-27.IX 1942 * MAX 26.IV 1880 MARKÉTA 18.X 1
.88-1.X 1944 IDA 12.II 1888-4.X 1944 LEO 16.X 1905-25.IV 1945 * RICHARD 17.II 1890-4.VIII 1942 * RUDOLF 23.IV 1880-4.VIII 1942 * RUDOLF 18.III 1886-9.II 1942
ZOFIE 1.III 1880-16.X 1942 * VIKTOR 9.V 1898-28.X 1944 * VILÉM 29.XI 1883 IRMA 17.X 1892 EVA 22.III 1925-26.III 1942 * VILÉM 7.III 1889-28.X 1944 * VI
* ALŽBĚTA 29.II 1860-19.X 1942 * AMÁLIE 27.II 1868-19.X 1942 * ANDĚLA 11.III 1869-28.XII 1942 * AUGUSTA 26.IX 1864-29.XI 1942 * AUGUSTE 4.X 1890
.IX 1943 * FRANTIŠKA 2.V 1886 MARKÉTA 12.III 1920-6.IX 1943 * FRANTIŠKA 5.XI 1900-16.X 1942 * FRIDA 5.VII 1880-4.VIII 1942 * HEDVIKA 7.XI 1874
.885-13.X 1941 VALERIE 15.X 1904-1.IV 1942 * VĚRA 16.X 1921-18.V 1944 * POPPOVÁ FRANTIŠKA 15.XII 1899-10.III 1943 * POR MAXMILIÁN 19.
.1942 * JOSEF 26.XII 1900-20.IV 1945 * AIL ADA 27.X 1909 RONAL D 11.VI 1934-6.X 1942 * JOSEF 17.XII 1901 HANUŠ 31.VII 1932-16.X 1942 * FRANTIŠEK 15.I 1904-
.1942 * OLGA 24.VIII 1886-19.X 1942 * OSKAR 31.VII 1901-24.IV 1945 * OTA 3.XI 1888 ELIŠKA 15.V 1896 PAVEL 15.V 1921 ARNOŠT 1.7.X 1927 25-6.IX 1942
VIII 1903-28.XI 1942 * RUDOLF 23.XI 1910-28.VIII 1942 * RUDOLF 24.II 1916 VĚRA 29.XI 1918-6.IX 1943 * VALTR 22.V 1901-15.XII 1943 * VLAST
.II 1922-9.III 1944 * JOSEFA 3.V 1876-19.X 1942 * JULIE 12.II 1859-19.X 1942 * JULIE 12.III 1863-19.X 1942 * KLÁRA 5.II 1897 LUDMILA 2.VIII 1922-4.VIII 1942 * AVAL
VLASTA 31.VIII 1899-4.X 1944 * PORIAS ADOLF 9.VII 1867-15.VIII 1942 * EDVARD 1.XII 1894-28.X 1944 * LEO 29.X 1893-31.III 1942 * PORTHEIM
IE 19.IV 1914 REGINA 15.IV 1906-8.X 1942 * POSNEROVÁ ANNA 24.X 1877-18.XII 1943 * POSTOLKOVÁ NORA 9.X 1914-14.X 1942
6 GISEL A 22.IX 1884-1.VIII 1942 * HELENA IV 1881-16.X 1944 * LUDMILA 11.X 1867-15.X 1943 * MARIE 23.X 1870-15.X 1942 * PRÁGROVÁ
ELA 8.XII 1907 ETEL 9.XI 1877-16.I 1942 * LUCIE 17.I 1914-11.III 1942 * PRESSLER FRANTIŠEK 26.II 1902-16.II 1942 * KAREL 25.XVI 1907-6.IX 1942
VI 15.VII 1883-26.XII 1942 * KLÁRA 18.IV 1897-17.IV 1942 * PRESSER ERVÍN 26.VII 1915-23.III 1942 * JAKUB 28.XII 1862-15.X 1942 * KAREL 29.X 1879
.PRINZ HERBERT 13.XI 1896-19.X 1942 * JOSEF 5.VIII 1875 HEDVIKA 12.II 1878-12.X 1942 * PRISANT ALEXANDR 2.X 1891-9.II 1942 * PRISKI
ERMÍNA 13.V 1894 HANA 11.VII 1921-15.I 1942 * JOSEF 1.VIII 1926-15.X 1943 * KAREL 8.XI 1890-11.XII 1942 * DORA 12.III 1897-28.V 1944 * PAVEL 18.VIII
RŮŽENA 4.VIII 1894-6.IX 1943 * PROSKAUER JINDŘICH JOSEF 30.VII 1901 PAVLA 23.IX 1900-12.III 1943 * OSKAR 13.VIII 1879 JANA 26.VII 1910
PŘIBRAM HUGO 6.I 1881-12.V 1942 * ROBERT 22.VI 1880-4.VIII 1942 * PŘIHODOVÁ ELA 20.IX 1903-29.III 1945 * PTÁČEK JAN 18.V
* NATAN 4.VIII 1878-2.III 1942 ZOFIE 16.X 1881-8.IX 1942 * PYROVÁ 2.VI 1892-20.XII 1943 * FRANTIŠKA 25.IX 1875-19.X 1942 * PYROVÁ O
.BINEK EMIL 17.IV 1878 JOSEFA 26.XII 1882-8.IX 1942 * RABINOVITZ MORIC 28.X 1896 MATYLDA 2.VII 1905 SIEGBERT 20.VII 1976
.1942 * RABL EMIL 24.VIII 1883 RŮŽENA 12.VII 1891-23.IX 1944 * JULIUS 14.VII 1872 FRANTIŠKA 1.XII 1874-19.X 1942 * MAX 15.X 1882 RŮŽ
* OTAKAR 15.III 1883 ERNA 26.VIII 1889-23.X 1942 * MARTA 23.X 1868-11.III 1942 * RADNITZER KAREL 29.VIII 1902-12.IV 1943 * HANA
.AX 19.XI 1866-26.XI 1943 * KAMILA 26.VII 1877-15.XII 1943 * RADOVIČIOVÁ LILY 11.I 1903-4.VIII 1942 * ADÉLA 16.IV 1878-28.VIII 1944
.I.IX 1878-15.XII 1943 * RAICHARTOVÁ JOSEFA 26.X 1916-? * RAIK ROBERT 28.VII 1902-24.III 1942 * RAIMANN VÍTĚZSLAV
1895-14.X 1944 * GUSTA 4.V 1892-15.V 1944 * SAMUEL 7.VI 1923-6.X 1942 * RANDA HERMAN 16.II 1878 GERTRUDA 29.V 1883-23.V
.23.II 1897-26.X 1942 * MAX 8.III 1884 BERTA 25.VIII 1887-6.IX 1943 * LOTKA 6.XII 1886-20.II 1942 * IRENA 11.I 1920-15.I 1942 * LILY 28.V 1892-4.VIII 1942 * RATI
.AUBITSCHEK ALFRED 13.XII 1895 ZDEŇKA 18.VII 1897-6.IX 1943 * JOSEF 8.VII 1922 OTAKAR 27.II 1892-11.III 1942 * VALTR 28.VII
.RŮŽENA 25.XI 1876-20.VII 1942 PERE 9.VII 1934 HANA 20.VI 1878-21.VII 1942 * GUSTAV 29.V 1900-22.I 1942 * ARNOLD 14.VIII 1884-6.IX 1943 * ARN
.ZENA 29.V 1899 JAN MICHAEL 23.II 1930-7.I 1942 * RAUCH DAVID 20.XII 1897 BOŽENA 26.VI 1900 RENÉ 17.VIII 1929-6.IX 1942 * EL
.RAWITZ JULIUS 1.IV 1888 ADELA 11.II 1900-11.III 1942 * RAYNALOVÁ RŮŽENA 11.XII 1871-10.VII 1942 * REACH ALOIS 4.II 1889-1.X 1942
.* ANNALIESA 3.II 1922-23.X 1942 * PAVEL 2.IX 1906-28.III 1945 VĚRA 6.X 1942 GÍTA 3.X 1941 MICHAL 6.II 1942-4.VI 1942 * RUDOLF 7.XII 1879 K
ETA 26.V 1879-22.IX 1942 * REBENWURZEL ARNOŠT 20.V 1912-6.IX 1943 * FRANTIŠEK 1.V 1906-28.II 1944 * KLÁRA 25.VIII 1904-6.IX 1944 * OTA
AMILIE 15.III 1942 * KAMILA 14.X 1874-15.X 1942 * KAROLINA 31.X 1908-22.X 1942 * REGINA 17.I 1879-4.VIII 1942 * REDISCH ARNO
43 * OTA 10.VIII 1882-22.II 1943 * ILSA 3.VII 1917 EDITA 31.V 1934-17.V 1942 * IRMA 6.X 1891-18.XII 1943 * JANA 6.VII 1876-19.X 1942 * RE DLING
.9.VII 1877-19.X 1942 * RECHT ALFRED 3.V 1897 HILDE 18.V 1911-30.V 1942 * LEO 28.IV 1929-17.V 1942 * RICHARD 22.V 1873-4.III 1944 * WIL
.S LEOPOLD 26.IX 1892 RŮŽENA 14.XII 1891 JIŘÍ 4.I 1926 LEO 28.IV 1929-17.V 1942 * REICH ADOLF 17.IV 1902 HERMA 11.IV 1911 ALŽBĚTA 9.IV 1
.EMIL 8.VIII 1887-27.III 1943 * ERICH 11.VII 1911-15.XII 1943 * PAVEL 15.I 1939-25.IX 1942 * GUSTAV 24.XII 1894 MILADA 3.VII 1909 JAN 20.V 1937-2
.OAL ŽBĚTA 17.I 1926-17.V 1942 * JOSEF 26.II 1910 PETR 9.IV 1938-15.V 1942 * JULIUS 3.I 1869 MALVÍNA 18.XII 1880 OTA 7.III 1914-16.X 1942
.1880-31.VIII 1942 * ELSA 21.III 1886-4.X 1944 * NATHAN 22.II 1877 BERTA 1.X 1880-21.X 1942 * OSKAR 18.XI 1876 IRMA 22.VI 1885-15.XII 1942
3.IX 1897 VALERIE 31.V 1905-9.I 1942 * VALTR 28.XI 1887 OLGA 25.X 1887 ZUZANA 25.X 1929-15.XII 1942 * VALTR 16.IV 1911-5.X 1943 * VA
.2.VIII 1882-26.X 1942 * HELENA 19.VIII 1881-12.V 1942 * IRMA 14.II 1886 PAVLA 1.V 1890-20.VIII 1942 * KAMILA 14.XII 1885-22.V 1942 * LAURA 16.VI
.ENBAUM ARTUR 12.XI 1896-31.III 1944 * HUGO 3.IX 1902 LUISA 8.III 1902-11.III 1944 * GRÉTA 16.V 1909-22.IX 1942 * RŮŽENA 25.III 1871-1
28.XII 1893-8.XII 1942 * KURT 25.V 1911 MARIANNA 14.II 1917-6.IX 1943 * LEOPOLD 24.X 1870-19.X 1942 * MAX 15.IV 1884 HILDA 16.IX 1896-6.IX
.ER PETR 15.V 1922-28.X 1942 * VILIAM 3.X 1900-6.IX 1943 * OLGA 16.XII 1867-17.IX 1942 * REICHMANN ALFRED 16.IX 1875-12.VII
.ILIÁN 23.VII 1900-6.IX 1943 * IRMA 31.X 1894-9.X 1942 * MOŘIC 3.X 1880 OTA 31.VII 1914 LOTA 15.XII 1878-25.IV 1942 * OTA 29.IV 1889-29
.VIKTOR 2.IX 1906-15.XII 1943 * ZDENĚK 26.XI 1900-3.III 1944 * KAMILA 28.VIII 1875-14.VII 1942 * RŮŽENA 24.I 1874-19.X 1942 * REICHSEEL
.2 EMIL 23.XI 1896 FRANTIŠKA 10.III 1906-17.V 1942 * FRANTIŠEK 16.IX 1890 ANNA 31.III 1894-26.IX 1942 * FRANTIŠEK 15.I 1879-10.X 1942 * MARIE 3
.IA 30-15.IX 1942 * KAREL 1.IV 1912-9.I 1942 * LEOPOLD 28.IV 1865-1.X 1942 * OTYLIE 15.X 1875-6.X 1942 * OSVALD 24.III 1884-16
.IX 1878-26.X 1942 * HERMÍNA 2.XII 1873-19.X 1942 * IDA 12.V 1878-12.X 1942 * MARTA 9.III 1882-26.X 1942 * REINAEROVÁ MARIE 17.XII
.X 1942 3 FELIX 27.IX 1904-19.X 1942 * ERVÍN 14.III 1904-16.X 1942 * FELIX 25.X 1880-13.VIII 1942 * FRANTIŠKA 17.X 1885-6.XII 1943 * HU
.AREL 13.I 1897-? * KAREL 1.XI 1916-6.X 1942 * KURT 25.VI 1929-16.X 1942 * LADISLAV 6.V 1883 HERMÍNA 11.XI 1885 MIROSLAV 4.V 1927
.* VÍTĚZSLAV 1.X 1879 MATYLDA 25.VIII 1877-17.V 1942 * ALICE 17.VII 1904-16.X 1942 * ANNA 16.VIII 1902 MARIE 19.V 1899-15.X
.A 31.II 1909-15.XII 1943 EVA 11.III 1940-20.II 1942 * HUGO 8.II 1881 RŮŽENA 17.XII 1881-12.V 1942 * JAROSLAV 16.V 1892-28.IX 1942 * EMA 31.V 1
.ATYLDA 12.X 1885-6.X 1942 * RUDOLF 1.XI 1880 ELIŠKA 10.II 1887-19.X 1942 * RUDOLF 5.IX 1900-15.XII 1943 * REINIS EMIL 30.VIII 1888 ELSA 1.X 1899 PAVA
.ELSA VI 1880-9.V 1942 * VILÉM 1916-6.IX 1943 * VIKTOR 1.XII 1875-2.V 1942 * KLÁRA 6.X 1895-9.III 1943 * ELSA 10.X 1942

FILIP 21.V.1885 ERNA 22.IV.1891 · 6.IX.1943 EVA 16.V.1941 · 15.IV.1943 FRANTIŠEK 5.IV.1873 · 28.V.1943 KAMILA 11.VI.1880 · 15.V.1944 FRANTIŠEK 31.
VII.1901 MANFRED 18.XI.1929 · 18.XII.1943 JIŘÍ 12.X.1923 · 18.XII.1943 JOSEF 29.II.1874 MARIE 21.III.1882 · 10.XII.1943 JOSEF 19.II.1889 ANNA 2.I.1886 · 17.II.1944
05·29.IX.1944 ALOIS 1.V.1908 · 22.X.1942 MOŘIC 26.VIII.1878 MAX 21.X.1880 VALERIE 22.XII.1909 · 6.IX.1943 OSKAR 12.XII.1879 · 28.IX.1944
1898·9.IV.1942 RUDOLF 11.IV.1909 ELA 3.VI.1911 · 6.IX.1943 RUDOLF 11.IV.1911 ANNA 26.VIII.1914 · 18.V.1943 VIKTOR 31.XII.1869 · 27.X.1944 VILÉM 2.
I.X.1943 HANUS 21.III.1915 · 26.X.1943 IRMA 4.IV.10.III.1887 · 28.VII.1942 KAROLINA 26.IV.1889 · 8.XII.1943 KAROLINA 9.
A 21.X.1884 · 9.III.1942 POLÁČEK JINDŘICH 12.III.1890 · 11.III.1942 POLÁŠEK ZIKMUND 13.V.1869 · 10.IV.1943 BEDŘIŠKA 10.I.1885 · 28.IX.1944 POLAI
R MICHAEL 15.VII.1885 · 26.VII.1942 ŠTĚPÁNKA 18.VIII.1888 IRMA 16.V.1885 · 12.III.1942 ARNOŠT 28.XI.1888 IRMA 16.V.1885 · 12.III.1942 ARNOŠT 2.IV.1911 · 7.III.1944 ARTUR 22.
4·6.X.1943 EMIL 2.VIII.1884 · 8.IV.1942 EMIL 5.III.1885 · 11.III.1942 EMIL 13.XII.1887 · 21.IV.1942 VALISKA 3.I.1902 · 20.VIII.1942 EMIL 4.XII.1897 · 10.III.1942 ARNOŠT 27.VII.1917 · 7.III.1944
I.IV.1977 · 15.IV.1943 · GERHARD 21.X.1907 · 31.I.1942 I LEO 6.V.1883 IRENA 5.XII.1894 · 22.IV.1942 GUSTAV 21.IX.1875 OLGA 29.VIII.1896 · 19.X.1942 HANU
2· HERMAN 24.I.1919 · 18.V.1944 HUGO 4.VII.1875 JILA 17.II.1881 · 22.X.1942 HUGO 5.III.1876 KAROLINA 21.V.1880 · 9.V.1942 HUGO 19.V.1907 · 1.IV.1943
HILDEGARDA 25.X.1907 · 9.X.1944 JIŘÍ 8.V.1891 · 12.X.1942 JIŘÍ 23.IV.1894 · 29.IX.1942 JOSEF 16.XII.1863 MALVINA 22.X.1870 · 25.IV.1943 · 6.IX.1943 · IV
893·11.III.1942 JOSEF 28.XI.1896 · 28.IX.1944 JOSEF 1.IX.1903 · 25.IV.1942 JOSEF 23.XII.1907 · 16.IX.1944 JOSEF 15.X.1920 REGINA 22.IX.1944
AREL 19.V.1923 · 13.VII.1942 KURT 20.V.1909 ELA 22.VIII.1938 · 15.IV.1943 LEO 13.XII.1875 IDA 18.III.1878 · 15.XII.1943 LEO 26.XII.1886
RIC 16.X.1898 ALŽBĚTA 11.III.1901 PETR 4.V.1937 · 28.IX.1944 OSKAR 18.XII.1887 ELSA 16.X.1897 · 21.X.1943 OSKAR 21.III.1882 ROBERT 28.VIII.1882 · 9.X.1942
OTA 22.VI.1894 · 11.III.1942 OTA 13.IX.1915 · 30.VI.1943 KAMILA 3.I.1889 · 15.V.1944 OTA X.1896 ANNA 23.VII.1877 · 12.X.1942 PAVEL 4.VIII.1894 · 7.
III.1942 · RUDOLF 22.III.1883 BERTA 6.VIII.1890 · 8.X.1942 RUDOLF 15.IV.1883 OTA 12.X.1885 · 6.X.1944 RUDOLF 2.VII.1884 KATERINA 15.
A 7.IV.1911 1901 · 28.IX.1944 RUDOLF 16.XII.1923 · 2.IV.1943 SAMUEL 6.VII.1859 · 9.V.1942 SAMUEL 1.XI.1876 · 18.V.1943 ŠTĚPÁN 13.XII.1913
· 9.IV.1943 VILÉM 11.V.1909 · 28.VII.1942 VILÉM 29.IV.1915 · 26.X.1942 HANA 15.II.1920 · 6.IX.1943 VALTR 30.X.1904 · 22.VII.1942 ANNA 12.VIII.19
GE 4·18.III.18.XII.1942 ALŽBĚTA 15.VIII.1865 · 6.III.1942 ALŽBĚTA 11.VIII.1887 · 8.X.1942 MARKÉTA 15.VI.1896 · 20.II.1942 ELEONORA 25.XII.1896
I.V.1920 · 17.III.1942 BEDŘIŠKA 8.V.1885 · 18.XII.1943 BEDŘIŠKA 5.XI.1886 · 6.IX.1943 BEDŘIŠKA 11.VIII.1890 · 1.IX.1942 BEDŘIŠKA 26.V.1896
2· EMILIE 22.XI.1875 · 19.X.1942 EMILIE 26.X.1877 · 4.VIII.1942 FRANTIŠKA 31.V.1873 · 19.X.1942 FRANTIŠKA 25.X.1873 · 22.X.1942 FRANTI
2III.1942 · HEDVIKA 12.XI.1895 ALICE 2.I.1925 HANA 6.II.1876 · 15.VI.1944 HEDVIKA 13.I.1900 KAREL 15.III.1929 · 4.X.1942 · HEDVIKA
2IF· JOSEFA 21.III.1880 · 14.VII.1942 JUDITA 22.VI.1890 OLGA 3.XII.1892 · 19.X.1942 KAMILA 6.IV.1871 · 19.X.1942 KAMILA 3.VII.1874 · 5.VIII.1942 · KAMILA
ARIA 13.VI.1875 · 19.X.1942 MARIA 15.IV.1880 · 15.V.1944 KAREL 17.XII.1910 · 11.VII.1943 MARIA 11.IX.1884 · 28.XII.1943 MATYLDA 11.V.1877 · 28.IX.1944 MILADA 11.V
26.X.1942 RŮŽENA 11.VI.1860 · 8.X.1942 RŮŽENA 16.IX.1863 · 19.X.1942 RŮŽENA 21.X.1893 ARNOŠT 25.XII.1915 · 15.V.1944 RŮŽENA 12.VII.1900 ŠTĚPÁN 19.XII
42· POLLATSCHEK ARNOŠT 5.VII.1896 · 28.IX.1944 ARNOŠT 22.III.1892 · 11.III.1942 ANTONIE 22.V.1903 · 25.IV.1942 CERTA
KÉTA 13.VIII.1878 · 12.X.1942 MELANIE 3.XII.1870 · 19.X.1942 POLLENZ ERVIN 12.V.1885 GRÉTA 1.VII.1882 · 15.II.1942 LEO 18.IX.1878 · 1.XIV.1942 PO
POLLNAUER JOSEF 19.I.1885 · 23.IX.1942 POLLONSCHII DAVID 1.VIII.1880 · 25.IV.1942 POLNAUER BEDŘICH 28.II.1879 · 6.IX.1
EDRICH 12.XII.1908 · 2.V.1942 JAN 3.II.1902 · 8.X.1942 ZOFIE 13.VIII.1889 ANNA 3.XII.1883 · 15.V.1944 POPOWSKY PAVEL 5.V.1910
· 9.V.1942 BEDŘICH 24.X.1907 HERTA 18.V.1913 · 12.X.1942 BEDŘICH 8.V.1908 · 6.XIV.1943 FRANTIŠEK 29.V.1915 · 28.IX.1944 BERTOLD 24.VII.1877 · 6.II
893·18.V.1942 ERVIN 21.X.1903 · 22.VII.1943 EVŽEN 28.III.1892 AURA 17.V.1897 · 15.V.1944 RUDOLF 28.VI.1875 · 11.VII.1943 FRANTIŠEK 14.V.1886 OLGA
AVEL 12.VI.1934 · 18.IV.1942 HANUS 22.IV.1911 JIŘÍ 6.XII.1920 · 3.VIII.1942 HUGO 1.XI.1881 HELENA 11.IV.1886 · 22.X.1942 HUGO 30.XII.
· 20.VIII.1942 JIŘÍ 20.IV.1908 · 18.V.1944 · STR 29.I.1978 · 28.X.1942 · JOSEF 10.III.1871 · 19.X.1942 · JOSEF 1.V.1874 KAROLINA 22.III.1876 · 15.V.1944
1 21.X.1892 ANNA 15.IV.1896 · 22.VII.1942 KAREL 16.X.1898 MILADA 2.III.1907 SON JAN 28.V.1913 · 1.IX.1942 KAREL 30.XI.1899 18.V.1944 KAREL 5.III.19
ŘÍC 7.II.1875 MARKÉTA 24.XI.1882 · 22.X.1942 MOŘIC 26.X.1889 11.V.30.III.1942 PETR 4.III.1939 · 20.VIII.1942 OSKAR 23.VII.1878 ELSA 12.X.1882 · 28.IX.1944 ELSA 11.
888· 25.IV.1944 IDA 18.VIII.1888 · 6.X.1944 RUDOLF 7.I.1889 ELISKA 13.I.1896 · 30.IV.1942 RUDOLF 25.I.1907 · 4.VIII.1942 JIŘÍ 18.XII.1921 · 26.X.1942 F
VII.1901 HANA 21.V.1929 · 4.VIII.1942 VILÉM 24.V.1898 HILDA 8.VIII.1895 ALFRED 7.III.1919 KAREL 4.XII.1925 · 4.VIII.1942 VILÉM 11.X.1898 ŠTĚPA
26.X.1942 BEDŘIŠKA 15.VIII.1878 · 4.VIII.1942 BERTA 22.V.1882 · 17.V.1942 BERTA 28.XII.1871 · 23.V.1942 EDITA 2.IV.1921 · 11.III.1942 ELIŠKA 8.VIII.1901 ·
IDLA 5.VIII.1879 · 26.I.1942 WOLFGANG 2.VII.1923 · 15.XII.1943 HEDVIKA 6.V.1886 · 19.X.1942 HELENA 29.X.1884 · 15.V.1944 HELENA 11.VII.1900 · 6.X.1944 · F
95· JIŘÍ 2.XII.1923 · 6.IX.1943 MARKÉTA 22.IX.1891 ANNA 6.II.1922 · 1.IX.1942 MARKÉTA 16.IX.1895 JINDŘICH 2.IV.1978 · 28.X.1944 MARKÉTA 13.V.1904 · 16
REGINA 22.V.1886 · 15.V.1944 VOJTĚCH 17.I.1896 MARKÉTA 10.III.1897 · 7.VII.1944 ZUZANA 29.III.1932 · 30.IV.1942 · PORCES ADOLF 23.X.1901 · 11.III.1942 ALF
ARTÍŠEK 14.VI.1908 · 6.IX.1943 HANUS 22.V.1899 · 25.VIII.1942 I HANUS 26.I.1908 VALERIE 23.III.1905 · 6.IX.1943 HUGO 7.IV.1857 · 27.VII.19
ATAK.III.1889 EDITA 8.V.1915 JOSEF 31.X.1920 · 15.IV.1942 KAREL 24.X.1899 ROBERT 2.VII.1917 REGINA 15.IX.1904 · 8.IX.1942 KAREL 11.VII.1909 ·
S·28.IX.1944 OTA 2.VII.1889 · 29.IX.1944 OTA 25.VI.1905 · 28.IX.1944 EDITA 8.VIII.1913 · 16.X.1944 OTA 4.X.1923 · 6.IX.1943 RICHARD 25.V
7· VILÉM 8.VIII.1909 ELSA 3.VIII.1904 · 19.X.1942 ALICE 15.XII.1904 · 19.X.1942 ALICE 11.VII.1870 · 18.VII.1942 ANNA 21.IX.1908 · 1.IX.1942 BERTA 11.X.1863 · 12.VII.1942 E
· RUDOLF· MALVINA 1.XI.1878 · 6.IX.1943 OTILIE 17.IX.1874 · 19.X.1942 MALVINA 8.V.1895 ALEXANDR 2.X.1915 · 3.IX.1942 MARIE 17.II.1885 GERTRUDA 12.XII
858·19.X.1942 EMIL 14.IV.1857 · 5.VIII.1942 EDUARD 15.X.1910 · 20.IV.1942 POSELES BERTOLD 18.X.1879 · 9.V.1942 POSENER VÍTĚZSLAV 2.
· JINDŘIŠKA 30.V.1891 · 12.X.1942 PRAGER BEDŘICH 21.IV.1900 · 9.I.1942 ERVIN 11.IV.1899 · 28.IX.1944 FRANTIŠEK 28.VIII.1897 J
891·26.X.1942 PRAŽÁK ALFRED 25.XI.1880 · 3.VIII.1942 ŠTĚPÁNKA 22.X.1885 · 18.V.1944 VERA 8.V.1911 KVĚTA 29.IV.1918 · 1.III.1942 Z DE
29.IV.1942 HILDEGARDA 16.V.1905 · 6.IX.1943 PREMITKL MENDL 5.III.1875 IRMA 6.V.1897 HANUS 16.III.1875 VERA 14.VI.1926 IRENA 17.V.1929 · 26
VII.1942 · VILÉM 22.IV.1861 · 19.X.1942 VALERIE 27.I.1896 · 19.X.1942 VERA 12.VII.1876 · 26.X.1942 PRIESTER EMIL 16.X.1897 · 23.I.1943
11.XI.1906 · 25.IV.1942 PROBST EMIL 22.XI.1889 FRANTIŠKA 9.IV.1884 LILY 17.VII.1919 · 4.VIII.1942 IZÁK 8.X.1873 · 15.XII.1943 PROCHÁZKO
· 19.X.1942 ANTONÍN 29.IV.1940 · 15.V.1944 RUDOLF 27.X.1888 REGINA 22.VI.1899 · 6.IX.1943 ZDENĚK 20.VI.1910 ANNA 30.XI.1908 · 18.XII.1943
OSSNITZ BEDŘICH 23.XII.1896 MARIE 6.X.1897 JINDŘICH 28.VI.1926 · 22.IV.1942 EMIL 22.IV.1879 · 4.VIII.1942 KAMILA 28.VII.1883 · 4.VIII.1944
DISLAV 4.XI.1892 · 20.VII.1942 PTIC EMANUEL 18.II.1892 CHAJA 18.IV.1899 · 18.X.1944 EDUARD 12.III.1915 · 6.IX.1943 PUDLES SALOMO
QUITTNER GUSTAV 12.III.1879 RŮŽENA 5.II.1883 · 6.IX.1943 LEO 7.IX.1894 · 16.I.1942 OSKAR 29.IX.1905 · 22.IV.1942 RAAB ALFRED
· ALFRED 16.XII.1874 · 4.III.1944 · EDUARD 12.II.1877 OLGA 5.XI.1881 · 28.X.1943 LILY 17.II.1916 · 18.XII.1943 FRANTIŠEK 18.IX.1909 ·
VII.1942 ZDENĚK 12.VII.1911 ARIANA 4.IV.1942 MARIANA 14.IX.1934 · 6.IX.1943 HANA 27.V.1869 · 18.XII.1943 RACENBERGOV
43· RADO ALEXANDER 14.XII.1913 BARNABAŠ 12.IX.1920 · 22.VII.1942 ARMIN 31.XII.1885 KLÁRA 19.XII.1889 · 9.V.1942 ELSA 21.VIII.19
AREL 23.VIII.1901 · 28.XII.1943 OTA 22.I.1898 · 19.X.1942 RAFALOVIČ SAMOIL 6.V.1882 PAV A 29.IX.1896 OLGA 3.III.1921 · 16.I.1942 Z
942· ANNA 2.XI.1893 · 15.XII.1943 ANNA 11.IX.1903 ZDENKA 15.V.1917 · 6.IX.1943 REGINA 2.III.1884 · 4.VIII.1942 RANSCHBURG HANUS 2.V.1925 · 28.IX.1944 RANZENHOFER HANUS 29.V.1910 · 23.X.1944 RE
JB·2· MENDEL 7.II.1872 · 14.VII.1942 SZ A 16.III.1895 · 18.V.1942 STEPHANIE 23.VIII.1875 · 9.I.1942 RATHAUS ELIÁŠ 26.XII.1872 · 4.IX.1942 RATHOUSKÁ KVĚTA 25.X.
O.VIII.1942 ARTUR ? 1896 · 4.XII.1941 ERICH 15.III.1875 · 2.I.1942 GABRIELA 3.I.1887 · 6.XII.1942 JENY 25.XI.1862 · 19.X.1942 LUDMILA 21.XI.1853
15.XII.1943 IRMA 19.XI.1885 ALICE 11.XII.1904 VERA 27.III.1937 · 15.XII.1942 RAUCHENBERG HERMAN 16.VI.1870 · 30.I.1944 JA
24· 4.X.1942 BEDŘICH 18.X.1898 ILKA 23.VII.1898 · 26.I.1942 FRANTIŠEK 7.II.1928 · 5.III.1942 PETR 9.VI.1930 · 26.I.1942 LEON 6.III.1910 · 6.IX.1943
· 26.X.1942 VIKTOR 27.III.1884 GISELA 19.XI.1879 KAREL 7.XI.1900 · 21.X.1943 ZIKMUND 21.X.1905 MARTA 10.IV.1905 · 26.X.1942 HERMÍNA
1945· REDERER ALFRED 19.VII.1888 HERMÍNA 30.IX.1896 · 8.IX.1942 · EDWARD 20.IX.1883 IRMA 5.VII.1898 · 18.V.1944 FRANTIŠEK 25.III.19
·· LOTAR 24.III.1900 MARIE 3.I.1876 · 8.IX.1942 MARIE 23.VIII.1895 · 6.IX.1943 REDLICH BERTOLD 20.VIII.1884 ELA 5.VII.1890 · 18.XII
1892· 31.VII.1943 BERTA 8.I.1901 · 6.IX.1943 REDNEROVÁ EDITA 1.VII.1917 TOMÁŠ 19.VI.1940 · 1.IV.1942 REGNER MAXIMILIAN 21.XII
ŘIŠKA 16.VI.1904 · 15.V.1944 LUISA 6.II.1888 IVO 17.I.1937 · 15.V.1944 JINDŘIŠKA 3.X.1908 IVO 17.I.1937 · 15.V.1944
LFRED 15.I.1915 · 6.IX.1943 ARNOŠT 6.V.1890 · 25.X.1943 EMA 16.XI.1885 · 23.X.1943 ARNOŠT 3.VIII.1915 · 15.XII.1943 BEDŘICH 11.II.1870 AN
AN 24.XI.1884 · 26.XII.1943 JAKUB 22.III.1890 VALERIE 12.XII.1889 · 15.V.1944 JAROSLAV 14.V.1898 HILDA 30.III.1896 RENEE 28.VIII.1931 · 1.IV.19
98· EMILIE 22.III.1890 · 17.V.1942 KAREL 19.V.1882 AMÁLIE 29.VI.1889 RUDOLF 12.IV.1928 MILOŠ 6.XII.1921 OTAKAR 4.III.1921 · 17.V.1942 KARL
3 OTO 16.XI.1897 · 1.IV.1942 OTA 10.X.1888 RŮŽENA 12.XI.1895 · 5.X.1942 IRENA 17.II.1897 · 30.IV.1942 EL 11.X.1901 · 29.IX.1944
1901 PETR 3.X.1978 · 12.IV.1942 VILÉM 20.VIII.1896 · 1.IX.1944 ANEŽKA 18.X.1884 · 19.X.1942 ANNA 23.I.1891 ARNOŠT 25.XI.1914 · 7.III.1944
MARIE 12.I.1867 · 21.VII.1942 MARIE 27.XII.1867 · 15.V.1944 MARKÉTA 14.VII.1902 · 15.V.1944 OLGA 11.VIII.1875 · 25.VII.1942 ZDENKA 6.VII.1886 ·
HER ARTUR 17.VII.1896 · 23.X.1944 VALERIE 27.X.1900 · 1.XII.1942 KURT 6.IV.1928 · 28.X.1944 EMIL 21.XII.1880 · 25.VII.1942 FERDINAND 2.VIII.1868
·6·17.I.1944 RUDOLF 19.VIII.19 TEREZA 26.I.1906 · 13.XII.1942 ZIKMUND 13.XII.1868 · 19.X.1942 REGINA 12.II.1878 · 25.VII.1944 REICHFELD
1894· 17.V.1942 EFRAIM 2.XII.1888 GERTRUDA 22.III.1904 · 15.XII.1943 ERICH 20.V.1912 · 27.III.1942 FELIX 28.II.1887 MARIE 28.IX.1888 · 15.V.1944
· 30.VII.1895 · 22.VII.1942 VALTR 5.XII.1905 · 6.IX.1943 VILÉM 24.XI.1891 · 23.IX.1943 VÍTĚZSLAV 27.III.1880 · 12.V.1942 ALŽBĚTA 11.V.1905 · 22.X.1942 VI
INA 21.XII.1910 · 22.VII.1942 REIK BEDŘICH 12.VII.1895 · 15.V.1944 BRUNO 20.IV.1892 · 9.I.1942 IRMA 23.VIII.1886 · 18.V.1944 KAREL 3.XII.1879 · 27.VII.1942 MARIE 17.V.1892 · 31.
RT 18.VII.1923 · 28.VII.1942 PAVEL 18.III.1899 · 1.IX.1942 RUDOLF 15.X.1873 · 17.V.1942 VIKTOR 10.VII.1892 GISELA 10.IV.1887 EVA 5.IV.1926 · 2
ARTUR 9.III.1885 KATERINA 29.VII.1907 PETR 4.IX.1925 · 17.V.1942 JOSEF 13.V.1912 · 6.IX.1943 LEOPOLD 5.X.1900 · 31.VII.1942 OTA 5.XI.1882
3A 3.XI.1878 · 15.V.1944 HUGO 2.VI.1882 PAVLA 25.I.1890 · 17.V.1942 HYNEK 15.V.1860 · 10.XI.1942 JAKUB 30.I.1868 · 26.IV.1942 JAKUB
OLD 14.VII.1878 KAMILA 6.X.1883 · 26.X.1942 LEOPOLD 5.I.1885 · 26.IV.1942 JAHA 26.VIII.1897 · 15.V.1944 NACHMANN 14.XI.1895 BERTA 14.VII.
1861·17.V.1942 EDITA 6.XI.1898 · 17.V.1942 HEDVIKA 8.III.1875 · 28.X.1942 HELENA 11.VIII.1898 · 6.IX.1943 HERMÍNA
VA FELICE 21.VI.1881 · 17.V.1942 REINISCH ALEXANDER 22.XI.1885 OLGA 8.III.1884 HANA 19.XII.1915 · 19.X.1942 ALEXANDER 22.XI.1906 A
JAROSLAV 14.XI.1880 · 15.V.1944 JIŘÍ 21.XI.1905 · 6.IX.1943 · JIŘÍ 22.I.1906 · 15.V.1944 JIŘÍ 6.VI.1913 HANA 13.XI.1896 · 18.XII.1943 JOSEF 18.VII.1870
78·17.V.1942 ANTONIE 22.IV.1864 · 26.X.1942 AUGUSTA 22.XII.1872 · 6.II.1943 HANA 11.VII.1910 · 12.III.1942 HERMÍNA 2.VI.1881 · 20.VIII.19
·· KAREL 5.XI.1883 · 2.I.1942 KAREL 18.XI.1890 · 15.V.1944 OSKAR 9.VIII.1886 RŮŽENA 11.XI.1897 ZDENĚK 11.VII.1926 · 23.I.1942 RE
1895·15.V.1942 JOSEFINA 2.V.1880 · 26.X.1942 REISENAUEROVÁ JOSEFA 5.VIII.1883 · 17.V.1942 REISER ADOLF 16.I.1884

But this was still life, and the end hadn't yet arrived. Even in this fortress town with walls shaped in the form of the star and behind the barbed wire, people still tried to lighten their lives with bits of sugar or a theater play. Yet, they were controlled by criminals who ruled over and judged them. Sometimes they were beaten and punished out of boredom and caprice of those in power.

On 10 January 1942, nine executions were carried out in Terezín as directed by camp Commandant Seidl. People had been sentenced to death for petty offences. They sat locked in the guardhouse. It took a long time to find a hangman, until a former assistant to the Prague executioner volunteered. A committee of elders and Czech police was forced to attend along with members of the SS. The rope to which one of the condemned had been tied broke; thus one of the condemned was left alive, and as was the custom in the First Republic, the hangman announced a stay of execution. However the leader of the camp ordered that the condemned man be hanged again. The condemned died bravely. When the SS men left the site of the execution, only members of the council of elders and police remained; the chief of police decreed, "Salute the executed."

LET THE GROANING OF THE PRISONER COME
BEFORE THEE; ACCORDING TO THE GREATNESS
OF THY POWER, SET FREE THOSE THAT ARE
APPOINTED TO DEATH.
-- Psalms 79:11

The end came quietly. The end meant further transports like the one that had brought them the fortress city, this time to an unknown country referred to as the East. And the East was an evil word, a word people feared. They did not know that where they are sending them flames from fiery ovens burned bright, even in the light of day. They did not know that a gas called zyklon would hiss its way into tiled rooms. They knew it was bad there, that they were closer to death. So they tried to stay in the fortress city, they thought up the most unlikely schemes to stay, to evade the transports. However, few were able to do so.

On 9 January 1942, the first transport left Terezín headed eastward to Riga. Out of 1,000 people transported, only 102 ever returned home. On 11 March, 1,001 left for Izbice, only 6 returned. On 17 March, another transport left for Izbice with 1,000 people, 3 returned. On 1 April 1,000 people left for Piask, 4 returned. On 18 April 1,000 people left for Rejnovice, only 2 returned. On 23 April 1,000 left for Lublin, only 1 returned. On 26 April 1,000 people were transported to Warsaw, only 8 were left alive. On the twenty-seventh of April another transport of 1,000 people was dispatched to Izbice, only 1 returned. On 28 April 1,000 people left for Zamošč, only 5 were left alive. On 13 April another transport of 1,000 people left for Zamošč, 19 people returned. On 9 May 1,000 people left for Ossov, none of them returned. On 17 April a transport of 1,000 people was sent to Lublin, not

one was left alive. On 25 April another
1,000 people were sent to Lublin, and 1 returned.
On 12 June 1,000 people were sent to Travniky, none
returned. On 13 June another 1,000 people were sent
off to a place unknown, no one knows their fate. On
14 July another 1,000 people were sent to Trostinec,
only 2 returned. On 28 July another transport of
1,000 people was sent to an unknown destination,
not one returned. On 1 September, a transport of a
thousand people was sent to Rassika, 49 returned.
On 8 September 1,000 people were sent to Trostinec,
only 4 returned. On 10 September, another transport
left for Trostinec, in it were 2,000 people, none
returned. On 22 September, 2,020 were sent to
Trostinec, none returned. On the 22nd of September,
1,000 people left for Minsk, only 1 remained alive.
On 23 September, a further transport of 1,980 left
for Trostinec, none returned. On 26 September
yet another transport of 2,004 people left for
Trostinec yet again, none remained alive. On
5 October 1,000 people were sent to Treblinka,
2 returned. On 18 October another 1,000 were sent
to Treblinka, 2 returned. On 28 October 2,018 people
left for Treblinka, none returned. On 6 October the
first transport of 1,866 people left for Auschwitz,
28 remained alive. That was the year 1942. In the
following years the transports continued, with
greater or lesser frequency. The last transport was
dispatched from Terezín on 23 October 1944.

WHAT PROFIT IS THERE IN MY BLOOD,
WHEN I SHALL GO DOWN TO THE PIT?
SHALL THE DUST PRAISE THEE?
SHALL IT DECLARE THY TRUTH?
-- Psalms 30:10

As more and more people kept leaving for nothingness, the numbers of people in the fortress town was dwindling. They showed them to a commission from the Red Cross who did not see anything, nor did they want to. They were shown paths filled in with sand, scrubbed sidewalks, a building labeled "school," a musical pavilion in the park, a café and a hospital. Everything had been thought out beforehand, everything was practiced and rehearsed. That day there was plenty of meat, though nobody got any. The meat was only for display. It was borrowed from the kennel, where the dogs had a right to real meat.

In honor of the Red Cross the children learned and performed a children's opera, Hans Krása's Brundibár. The Red Cross commission and the SS were very pleased by the children's performance as well as with the director and composer. After the commission had left, all those who had performed were dispatched to Auschwitz where they died in the gas chambers.

AND I WILL CUT OFF THE CITIES
OF THY LAND, AND I WILL THROW DOWN
ALL THY STRONG-HOLDS
-- Psalms 5:10

RŮŽENA 7.II 1877-28.X 1944 * SELMA 19.VII 1877-15.XII 1943 * LACHMANN Pavel 25.VI 1896-6.IX 1943 * LACHS VIKTOR 5-3.XII 1941 * LAMMELOVÁ BERTA 8.III 1877-28.X 1944 * LAMPEL JIŘÍ 24.II 1891 JOSEFA 16.XI 1893-9.IX 1942 26.XI 1942 * LACHS VIKTOR 1898-29.IV 1944 HILDA 2.II 1908 ZELIN 21.V 1931-4.X 1944 * JULIUS 13.VI 1884 ERNA 12.III 1899 ERIK 2.III 1925 GERDA 16.II 1927 * RENEE 26.I 1937 * HELENA 8.XII 1909-20.IV.3 NELY 8.VII 18-.IX 1942 * IDA 5.VI 1873-9.IX 1942 * KAMILA 15.XII 1885-21.III 1942 * MARIE 16.XI 1902 DORI 42 * OSKAR 5.I 1897-3.III 1944 HEDVIKA 21.X 1944 JIŘÍ 15.IV 1923-8.V 1944 SONJA 15.VII 1928-22.IX 1943 * OLGA 29.VII 1904-11.II 19 MARTA 20.II 1911-6.XI 1944 * JULIUS 4.VI 1869 MARIE 7.XII 1879-18.XII 1943 * LANDSMANN BEDŘICH 27.XII 1881-4.VIII 1942 * VIKTOR 12.II VI 1896 MARIE 1.XI 1903 HANA 6.IV 1927 MILAN 3.I 1932-26.I 1942 * HANUŠ 26.I 1898 JULIANA 25.III 1904 G

Rudolf 31.II 1896-29.VII 1944 * KAMIL 25.III 1905-31.XII 1944 * LAVIČKOVÁ ANNA 7 1817-?

A mother's hands smoothing a child's hair, lovers' hands intertwined, hands blessing a chalice of wine, hands clasping a hoe, a hammer or a plane, the firm hands of doctors tending the sick, fine hands of an embroiderer, the hard and calloused hands of old men, the small fists of a child. And hands rising from graves, hands bloodied by wounds, a hand with nails torn and crushed by steel-toed shoes.

At roll call Dr. Mengele stood in his white coat making the selections. If he pointed his hand to the left, it meant life; if he pointed his hand to the right, it meant death. Women with children always went to the right, meaning death, while women without children went to the left, to live. A woman could spare her own life by giving up her own children. But none of the mothers did. They followed their children to the gas.

MINE EYES DO FAIL WITH TEARS, MINE INNARDS
BURN, MY LIVER IS POURED UPON THE EARTH,
FOR THE BREACH OF THE DAUGHTER
OF MY PEOPLE, BECAUSE THE YOUNG CHILDREN
AND THE SUCKLINGS SWOON IN THE BROAD
PLACES OF THIS CITY.
-- The Lament of Jeremiah, Lamentations 2:11

And ashes cover the land and rise to the heavens, millions burned in the ovens, and those 77,927 from my native land are only a drop in the ocean of dead from chared villages, razed cities and overturned graves. And the handful of those who survived see shadows, shadows of unburied loved ones whose ashes have been mixed into the earth. The shadows are silent, as if reproachful or on guard. However, their ashes mix into the fertile soil, good land from which crops grow and trees blossom. Walk through these lands where waters rush through rapids and pines whisper through the rocks, and beauty shines in the brightness of dawn as the shadows walk with you hand in hand. For in peace and serenity, it is their land, too.

On 17 March 1943 the so-called family camp at Auschwitz was liquidated. Eight thousand men, women and children were sent to gas chambers. They knew what fate awaited them, they knew they were going to their deaths. They went singing the anthem of their native land, "Where My Homeland Lies."

YET THEY ARE THY PEOPLE AND THINE
INHERITANCE, THAT THOU DIDST BRING OUT
BY THY GREAT POWER AND BY THY
OUTSTRETCHED ARM
-- Moses 9:29

p. 8   ...*that day* – This is March 15, 1939, when Czechoslovakia was partitioned, its western region invaded by the Wehrmacht and turned into an entity called the Protectorate of Bohemia and Moravia.

p. 23   *Reinhard Heydrich* (1902–1942) – one of the highest members of the Nazi leadership, also known for his active participation in the planning of the Holocaust. In September 1941 he was appointed Acting Reich-Protector of the so-called Protectorate of Bohemia and Moravia, where he immediately proclaimed martial law and ordered mass executions of members of the Resistance. He died in Prague as a result of an assassination in June 1942.

p. 23   *Terezín* (in German: *Theresienstadt*) – originally a garrison town built in the late eighteenth century as one of the military installations directed against the Habsburg Empire's northern competitor, Prussia. In the twentieth century it was a small township consisting mainly of old-fashioned military barracks. In late 1941, Terezín was converted into a holding facility for Jews, mostly from Bohemia and Moravia, whom the Nazis successively deported to extermination and concentration camps in occupied Poland, Belarus, Latvia, and Estonia. The Terezín "ghetto" served as a detention site until May 1945. In Czech, the word *transport* was mainly understood as deportation to Terezín.

p. 24   *exhibition grounds* – the infamous Radio Trade Fair in Prague, a facility where Jews called to deportation were commanded to report before being deported by trains to Terezín. The "registration" process was brutal and could last several days, despite the fact that accommodation facilities were absent, hence the note about people sleeping on concrete floors.

p. 38   *Red Cross mission* – As the war was coming to its final stages, the International Committee of the Red Cross succeeded in arranging an inspection in Terezín. This happened on June 23, 1944. Terezín was carefully "beautified" for this event so that the inspectors could not raise any objections to the poor living conditions. The "beautifications" were temporary and mostly faked. For details, see: https://encyclopedia.ushmm.org/content/en/article/theresienstadt-red-cross-visit

p. 38   *Hans Krása* – Hans Krása (b. 1899) was one of the Jewish composers deported to Terezín, where he was active in musical activities that the ghetto's administration tolerated. Among other things, he staged *Brundibár* [Bumblebee], an opera written for children actors, that was also shown to the Red Cross inspectors in an attempt to document a vibrant cultural life in the ghetto. Krása was deported to Auschwitz, where he perished on Oct. 17, 1944; for details see: http://holocaustmusic.ort.org/places/theresienstadt/

p. 41   *family camp (Familienlager)* – a special section of the Auschwitz concentration camp that held several transports of Jews from Terezín. It is not entirely clear what purpose was behind this installation, but conditions in it were slightly better, as families were not separated, hence the "family camp." Most inmates were eventually sent to gas chambers; this happened in two stages, on March 8–9, 1944, and July 10–12, 1944. Today, March 9 is commemorated as the National Day of Remembrance in the Czech Republic.

–jt

AFTERWORD:
NOTES ON AN OCCASIONAL PRINT

Taking the first edition of Jiří Weil's *Lamentation for 77,297 Victims* (1958) into one's hands, one might be inclined not to think of it as a real book. It consists of two signatures—that is, two folded sections of paper loosely inserted into a simple wrapper, no binding, just a few pages accompanied by three graphic plates by Zdenek Seydl. An occasional print? If so, what was the occasion?

The *Lamentation's* wrapper is based on a photograph of the wall from the Pinkas Synagogue in Prague. It shows a detail with names of Jewish victims of the Shoah from Bohemia and Moravia, to whom the title of Weil's homage refers. Those names and the corresponding dates of birth and death were at that time being inscribed on the expansive interior surfaces of this site by Czech artists Václav Boštík (1913–2005) and Jiří John (1923–1972). The connection between Weil's publication and the memorial project is asserted once again right on the first page of the text, where we read: "*All of the names* [of victims] *are being inscribed on the walls of the Pinkas Synagogue, which lies next to the Old Cemetery. Thus will their memory be preserved.*" The project of turning the Pinkas Synagogue into a site of Jewish memory had been in the planning since 1954, yet by the time Weil's *Lamentation* appeared in 1958 it was still far from finished. Still, in May of that year, visitors could have a glimpse—the state organized a country-wide "Week of Museums" and so the memorial was briefly accessible to the general public within the frame of this event. The official opening followed only in 1960.

The thin folder is thus most likely an occasional print, yet one that transcends the occasion at the same time. In early 1959, Rudolf Iltis, probably the first reviewer of Weil's *Lamentation*, noted the symbolic meaning of the cover when discussing the booklet, but he also suggested that Weil's *Lamentation* was an appropriate reminder of the night of March 8–9, 1944, the date when the inmates of the so-called *Familienlager* (family camp), a section of Auschwitz that segregated thousands of Jews deported from Bohemia and Moravia, were sent to the gas chambers. This was certainly a justified interpretation, since Weil's *Lamentation* refers to this mass murder repeatedly.

In 1958, Jiří Weil was a senior librarian at the State Jewish Museum in Prague. By this time, he had a long literary career behind him that was already well underway in the 1920s. Born in 1900, he was the author of several novels, numerous short stories, translations, journalism and essays about Czech Jewish history. He survived the war, in part in hiding, but now he was also a relatively fresh target of ideological purges conducted in the Czechoslovak Writers' Union in the early 1950s. What is now his best-known book, *Life with a Star* (1949), was withdrawn from

circulation. By the end of the 1950s he was finishing another novel set in Czechoslovakia's war period, *Mendelssohn Is on the Roof* (1960), and he played a significant role in a 1959 publication that collected children's drawings from Terezín/Theresienstadt, a detention ghetto for Jews in the so-called Protectorate Bohemia and Moravia. He was also publishing in Czech Jewish periodicals. In other words, Weil was at the peak of his career, yet leukemia terminated his efforts in 1959.

Born into the family of a small Jewish entrepreneur, Weil became an ardent admirer of the new Soviet state already in the early 1920s. He graduated with a degree in Russian literature, and both his engagement and expertise in Russian culture made the Czechoslovak Communist Party send him to the USSR in 1933, where he was active as a translator in the Comintern, a Soviet organization designed to coordinate the world's Communist movements from the very center, Moscow. He was lucky to have returned to Czechoslovakia three years later despite the fact that the Stalinist purges were just about to enter its intense phase. Soon after his return he published his novel *From Moscow to the Border* (1937), a title that would mimic destinations printed on a railway ticket. The novel is clearly biographical, setting the action at the onset of the brutal process of Stalinization and the era of the Great Purges. Liberal critics praised the book as revelatory; Communist critics were outraged. A sequel written in a similar tone, *The Wooden Spoon*, remained unpublished before the war. In 1939, Czechoslovakia fell apart.

Weil's oeuvre barely contains any references to Jews and Jewishness prior to 1939. This changed with the occupation years. Weil became a victim of antisemitic persecution in his own country, now dismembered and occupied. Among his stations was the Jewish Museum in Prague, which was, ironically enough, the site where dispossessed Jewish property was processed. Weil was eventually lucky to survive, refusing to follow the call to the concentration camp and spending the last months of the war in hiding. The occupation years transformed his work significantly, making Jewishness a tangible dimension of his oeuvre. This is reflected by the short stories he wrote while in hiding and collected under the name *Colors* (1946), but perhaps most visibly by his novel *Life with a Star,* which he still managed to publish in 1949, shortly after the 1948 Communist takeover in Czechoslovakia. Again, the story is based on experience. The main protagonist, a Jewish bank employee called Josef Roubíček, is gradually deprived of all his rights. Weil shows him as a marginalized character who is receiving ordinances that list places Jews are excluded from and things they are supposed to surrender—he must shop for groceries during designated hours only and may buy just a restricted array of goods, provided they are available at all; he must not own a radio, a typewriter, or musical instruments; he must not go to restaurants, concerts or movie theaters; he may not freely use street cars and trains. In other words, Weil does not write about Jewish suffering in concentration camps but focuses on the dehumanizing aspects of the marginalization of Jews that preceded their deportation, highlighting administrative measures that generated an enormous degree of debasement and anxiety. This process can easily be generalized beyond the fate of a specific community.

After the reviewers criticized his "unhealthy" subjectivism and formalist approach to writing, Weil was excluded from the Czechoslovak Writers' Union in the early 1950s. Indeed, echoes in *Life with a Star* of Franz Kafka and existentialism, including J.-P. Sartre's *Roads to Freedom,* were hardly welcome at a time when Socialist Realism was declared official cultural policy in Czechoslovakia. And an attack came even from within the Jewish community. As he had avoided deportation, he was not considered by some to be a real victim, and so he had no mandate to speak about Jewish suffering during the war. *Life with a Star* was quickly withdrawn from distribution—paradoxically so, since the novel's hero eventually decides to resist a call to the concentration camp and goes underground instead. He receives support from a working-class resistance group.

Weil's *Lamentation* represents a style of writing that is different from his previous prose. One is obviously struck by the way the text is composed and typographically executed. With a few ex-

ceptions, each page consists of three different sections, or layers: the top is a narrative of the Shoah in the Czech Lands, the middle is a set of personalized episodes featuring Jewish victims, and the section in the lower part is reserved for biblical quotes. Weil thus presents his reader with at least two options for reading his *Lamentation*. The reader can read the three sections on the page successively from top to down, continuing page by page until the end—let's call it the "vertical option"—or he may select one of the layers and pursue it across the entire book until its very end—let's call that the "horizontal option." If the reader takes the vertical option, the episode section and the biblical quotes enter a complicated relation with the top of the page. The episode paragraph in the middle becomes a "footnote" to the lead narrative, and the biblical quote becomes a spiritual commentary, perhaps on both of the paragraphs above it. If the reader takes the horizontal option, he transforms the text into three strips running all the way across the book. He may read the entire Shoah narrative as one piece, or go step by step through the collection of episodes, or try to find some overarching logic in the stream of biblical quotations in the third layer.

Whichever reading is chosen, each of the three sections has its own characteristics. The Shoah narrative uses the high style, in which the Czech reader will have no trouble recognizing the role of the Terezín Ghetto although its name is not named explicitly. This is Weil's own rendering of the events of the Shoah in the Czech Lands. He repeats motifs that are familiar from *Life with a Star*, starting with the day of occupation, continuing with details of deportation, and ending with an elegy for those murdered on the night of the *Familienlager* liquidation. We can note striking patriotism, particularly visible in the recurring motif of "my land," i.e., the Czech land. The motif is already present in Weil's earlier short stories, including those in the collection *Colors*. Crucially, however, the final lines almost seem to be directed at the non-Jewish reader. For Weil, shadows of the murdered are present after liberation, Jewish victims walk with the living hand in hand, because "This land is theirs, also" [Neboť i jejich je tato země]. The emphasis—and the reminder—is on *also*.

The middle section may seem to repeat Weil's Shoah narrative, since it begins and ends with the destruction of the *Familienlager* at Auschwitz. This section might be reasonably called the "episode strip," since it includes passages and episodes that claim facticity in stating names, dates and locations explicitly. Names of a few Nazis, such as Heydrich and Mengele, are not left out, either. These episodes are disturbing and almost surreal in depicting the deaths of Jews in the process of segregation and preparation for deportation. Recall, for instance, the suicide of Josef Friedman; the death of Rudolf Jakerle, who suffered a stroke after being unable to withdraw his pension from his bank account; the denouncement of Max Opperman, who was reported for attending a Beethoven concert; the fate of Rudolf Kohn, a disabled man, at the Radio Trade Fair; and a few others. Weil used some of them already in

Life with a Star, where they appear as a sort of "oral folklore" that Jews waiting for deportation were passing from one to another, but now the genre of lamentation propels them beyond the binary of facticity and fiction. While the Shoah layer shows emotions and depicts the perpetrators without pardon, the episode layer is largely cold and impersonal. And, again, it is patriotic. Weil describes the scene when inmates of the *Familienlager* are proceeding to gas chambers, singing. There are independent reports that they were singing both the Czechoslovak national anthem and the Jewish song Hatikvah, later the anthem of the state of Israel, but Weil chooses to depict the national anthem.

The final level of the horizontal reading consists of biblical quotations. This level is hard to read in a sequential manner across the entire book. Most of the quotes are taken from the Psalms, and they might be best understood as immediate reflections on what is above them on the page rather than a continuous narrative. It is perhaps only the opening and the final passages, both taken from Deuteronomy, that create an arc spanning across this section. Weil starts with Deuteronomy 28:45, which, however, had he quoted it in full, reveals a condition, that if God's commandments are not observed, misfortunes will follow: "They will pursue you and overtake you until you are destroyed, because you did not obey the LORD your God and observe the commandments and decrees he gave you." In shying away from the motif of God's wrath and punishment, Weil uses only the prophetic part about destruction and death to set the stage. He seems unwilling to accept the idea of guilt.

Significantly, the final quote, Deuteronomy 9:29, provides a resolution. It is taken from the pivotal moment in Moses's encounter with the Lord on Mount Sinai, when Moses successfully argues that Jews are worthy of support. Weil quotes Moses's plea to God: "But they [Jews] are your people and your legacy" (Deut. 9:29). This can be read as a reminder and a declaration of loyalty, or both. And, indeed, God is willing to "reissue" the tablets Moses had smashed, thus expressing trust. In other words, in the vertical reading this passage is a commentary on the death exemplified by the annihilation of the *Familienlager*, while in the horizontal

reading it represents a grand conclusion affirming the continuity of Jewish life. Weil was not a man of religion, but in placing this passage at the key point of his composition, he understood that it can and should be invoked.

Strictly speaking, we might ask whether Weil's is a lamentation at all. It is certainly different from the texts of mourning that we know from the biblical Book of Lamentation, which is about the destruction of Jerusalem by Babylon, and which Weil also uses in one instance. Lamentations have some tradition in the Bohemian Jewish context, though; the oldest that comes to mind is the penitential "All that Suffering," composed by Rabbi Avigdor Kara (d. 1439) for the victims of the pogrom that devastated Prague's Jewish Town in 1389. Kara assumed the style of a report of events, which lists episodes that claim authenticity, although he otherwisc follows a highly furmulaic genre and presents a fine rhetorical structure with more than two dozen biblical quotations. Importantly, Kara's lamentation evolved into a *piyyut*, a poem rc-cited during religious services, in this case during the afternoon service in Prague's Old-New Synagogue on Yom Kippur. Thus it assumes a strong performative quality.

Does Kara set a background for Weil? One could argue that parts of Weil's text also function as a report, and that there are similar details in the two compositions. Thus consider Kara's de-scription of the incursion into the ghetto:

> They rushed from one gate to another, used every opening,
> they gathered in bands and hordes,
> boosting their spirits with singing and wild shouts
> to shed pure blood and commit robbery.*

Similarly, Weil describes the Nazi invaders as coming with calls for violence and a desire to steal and loot:

> Death entered the city that day, accompanied by fifers,
> horsetail bearers, death's heads and the rattle of drums.
>
> (Weil, page 9 above)

But these are frequent motifs in pogrom narratives, after all. Differences are perhaps more important: while Kara used biblical passages directly in his text to show his command of a high rhetor-ical culture, Weil works with biblical language differently, giving it a new context in a separate section that, as we have seen, serves as a commentary on the others.

As Weil uses the Czech term *žalozpěv* in the title, literally a "sorrow song," a compound that parallels the German *Klagelied*, we might argue that the element of singing should move the text in the

---

* Translation based on David J. Podiebrad, *Alterthümer der Prager Josefstadt,* second ed., Prague 1862, p. 127.

direction of performance as well. "Songs of sorrow" are features of real-time rituals across cultures. Nonetheless, we do not have to think of the performative quality in the literal sense. Weil's is an act of homage verbalized by a survivor; it expresses mourning for those who perished without receiving the *kaddish*. And, perhaps most importantly, Weil introduces a new kind of performance: the visual dynamics rooted in the layout of the printed page. The solution he is proposing—a tripartite page—is absorbing. It is unique in its execution, yet at the same time it echoes liturgical literature, where a core passage may be flanked by commentaries and commentaries on commentaries. In Weil's arrangement, however, any section can be the core, and any other can be a commentary.

Placing Weil's *Lamentation* in the Czech literary context of the 1940s is certainly possible. Jiří Orten (Jiří Ohrenstein, 1919–1941), a young Jewish poet whose life was terminated in a bizarre traffic accident involving a Gestapo car in 1941, turned to laments in the months before his death, leaving behind a short private print entitled *Jeremiah's Lament* (1940) and a poetry collection *Elegies*, published posthumously in 1946. It is in the former text that we read lines of desperation with which he addresses God:

You covered yourself with the clouds and hid behind
$$\text{the waters,}$$
So you may not hear what I cry unto heaven,
And you veiled me, too, gave me the night which lets me think
That I must not fall asleep, that you will perhaps call me.

I listen all the time, you're quiet, like a deaf one.
I listen through tears, I listen, I hear nothing.

While Orten's lament may function as one of the reference points when reading Weil, the literary context of the 1950s may perhaps be more immediate, especially as regards the episode layer in Weil's *Lamentation*. Recall that this layer was meant to exemplify a mode of writing that claimed facticity while suppressing emotions or value judgements on the part of the author.

Such was also the program of Jiří Kolář (1914–2002), artist, poet, and Weil's close friend, with whom Weil was in steady contact in the 1950s. (Kolář dedicated his collection *The Eyewitness: Diary from the Year 1949* to Weil's memory.). Himself a Gentile author, Kolář was preoccupied with the violence of the war, including the Shoah. His works of the late 1940s and 1950s are perhaps best exemplified by the collection entitled *The Black Lyre*, which morphed several times to be eventually incorporated into his 1966 collection *The Aesop of Vršovice / 1954–57*. In this edition, *The Black Lyre* begins with a text titled "Marie Noušková," which presents recollections of a Czech woman-prisoner in the Ravensbrück concentration camp. She is understood to be a witness who is presenting non-literary testimony of inhuman conditions in the camp. Kolář may have appropriated this account directly from Noušková's raw manuscript. "Marie Noušková" is followed by a text titled "1944," which depicts the events in Auschwitz in 1944, including the annihilation of the *Familienlager*. Again, the text is based on a non-literary text, *The Death Factory*, a memoir by two Auschwitz survivors, Oto Kraus and Erich Kulka. That book, which has several Czech editions since 1946, goes into great details in depicting atrocities committed at Auschwitz, including the treatment of Jews from Bohemia and Moravia.

In a brief afterword, Kolář provides a commentary on his approach: "*The whole collection was meant to be a history of human evil* [podlost]*, concluding with testimonies from concentration camps. I first tried to 'move' these testimonies into the usual 'literary fog', but I soon became aware of the pointlessness of my efforts and decided to preserve their authenticity. That's why I called these poems 'authentic poetry.'*" Obviously, the program was to avoid poetic language.

Although Weil did not leave a comparable commentary, it is fair to claim that in one way or another Kolář and Weil converged on the program and practice of "authentic writing." This concept echoes the overall sentiment that is perhaps most familiar from Theodor W. Adorno's oft-quoted dictum about the impossibility of writing poetry after Auschwitz. Such was also the approach of other European authors who wrote about extermination camps; one may think of *This Way for the Gas, Ladies and Gentlemen* (1946; in English 1967) by the Polish author and Auschwitz inmate Tadeusz Borowski (1922–1951). In the grand scheme of things, these authors were pursuing the same goal. At the same time, however, their approaches differed considerably. Kolář was rewording found texts, for which he intervened by breaking standard prose paragraphs into short "poetic" lines. Borowski wrote his prose texts on the basis of his experience in Auschwitz and largely suppressed moral judgement. And Weil drew on narratives circulating among Prague Jews prior to deportation. At the same time, "authentic poetry" was just one of the options available to him; the Shoah narrative in his *Lamentation* is certainly not in this line. It is perhaps pointless to discuss the question of whether these authors escaped the inevitable paradox of estheticizing their subject matter by simply bracketing out their judgements. And it is perhaps equally unhelpful to reduce everything to one single program. A lamentation is rooted in a therapeutic need to speak out. Weil spoke out, thus constructing a space in which the Shoah could be discussed in a language that did not adhere to the expected ideological constraints.

To finish the story, we return to the Pinkas Synagogue. The building was closed to visitors in 1968. The fact that groundwater was seeping into the walls offered an easy pretext, and the endless line of names became inaccessible until 1990. The regime had no interest in a site of Jewish memory. In fact, parts of the walls were even chiseled away. Weil's *Lamentation* was not republished until the 1990s, either. Yet already at the time of its origin it represented an opening that helped (re)construct the memory of the Shoah. There is ample reason to record Weil's role in this process by way of a translation.*

Jindřich Toman,
Ann Arbor, MI

* The author is grateful to Petr Brod and Benjamin Paloff for comments on an earlier draft of this afterword.

SELECTED TEXTS BY JIŘÍ WEIL IN ENGLISH

Life with a Star (translated by Růžena Kovaříková [=Rita Klímová] and Roslyn Schloss, with a preface by Philip Roth, New York 1991); *Mendelssohn is on the Roof* (translated by Marie Winn, New York 1991); *Colors* (translated by Rachel Harrel, Ann Arbor, MI, 2002); with Hana Volavková, *I Never Saw Another Butterfly: Children's Drawings and Poems from Terezín Concentration Camp, 1942-1944,* New York 1978.

SELECTED SECONDARY LITERATURE
IN ENGLISH

Jiří Weil's work has been studied by a number of scholars in the Czech Republic, including Jiří Holý, Hana Hříbková, Alice Jedličková, Miroslav Kryl, Jan Podlešák, Eva Štědroňová, and others. Probably the first one who alerted the English-speaking readership was Philip Roth: note his foreword to *Life with a Star*. See also the doctoral dissertation about Jiří Weil by David Thomas Lightfoot, University of Toronto, 2002, and entries on Weil and post-Holocaust Czech-language literature by Jonathan Bolton in The YIVO *Encyclopedia of Jews in Eastern Europe* (online http://www.yivo.org/publications). Further see Jindřich Toman, "Jiří Weil," in *Holocaust Novelists*, ed. by Efraim Sicher, Detroit 2004, pp. 354–358.

Writing a translation is a huge responsibility, and in the case of *Lamentation for 77,297 Victims*, one that has weighed on me since I undertook my study of Weil some twenty years ago. It is an important work for readers of Weil in that it serves as a coda of his output, developing themes of alienation and dehumanization that span his career. It is also an important historical document that describes the crimes of the Nazi era in a way that I believe is unique. Weil's descriptions illustrate the forces that lead a society to mass murder – the transformation of neighbours and perhaps even friends from human beings into faceless numbers.

Weil's writing defends the value of the individual inversely to the political dehumanization he witnessed. His successful novel, *Life with a Star* (1949) narrates one man's painful decision to evade the Nazi transports of Jews from occupied Bohemia and Moravia to Terezín, a holding centre from which Jews were dispatched to concentration camps in other countries. The protagonist's reality is so harsh, so bitter, that he retreats into a dialogue with his own imagination, where he sees hope as a fairytale, and reality as an anti-Semitic joke. Yet when he meets a labourer who recognizes his humanity, his sense of self returns. He breaks free of the fairy-tale narrative and self-deprecating humour and allows himself to be put in the hands of workers who will protect him. Doing so, he is no longer a humiliated subject and victim of the evil invaders, but a human being, neither heroic nor cowardly, merely a man who wants to survive.

Life with a Star is not autobiographical, but it is informed by Weil's experience as one of only about 400 Czech Jews to survive the war by going into hiding (where he was aided by Franz Kafka's niece Věra Saudková among others). While some details about Weil's concealment are documented — he had feigned suicide by dropping a briefcase into the Vltava and screaming "a man is drowning" — he never revealed many of the details, even to close friends. We do know that Weil dreaded and feared for his life under

Nazi rule, yet he was shocked that he was singled out as a Jew rather than as a Communist.

Weil fought the Bolshevization of the Czechoslovak Communist Party, but remained a Communist until his expulsion from the Party (1935). He fell under suspicion again, as did most Czechoslovak Jews, during the Stalinism of 1949–1957.

Through the kindness of Josef Škvorecký, I was able to correspond with and meet Jiří Weil's surviving friends in 2000–2001. The first of these friends that I spoke with was Jiří Žantovský, a classmate from a famous gymnasium that educated the founders of Devětsil and the first generation of the Czech Avant-garde. Žantovský described him as a serious intellectual and a gifted writer, but also a *krajan*, a good old Czech, who enjoyed tramping in the countryside. He knew Weil from his most political days, but knew nothing of his Jewish identity.

Jiří Kolář and his wife Běla Kolářová, friends since Weil emerged from hiding in 1945, knew and admired Weil as a successful writer of the previous generation. Both Jiří's left the Communist Party of Czechoslovakia after the war, during the Stalinist purges and show trials of the Gottwald Era (Weil was expelled; Kolář left voluntarily). Unable to publish, Weil was rescued from manual labour when the Jewish Museum in Prague hired him as a cataloguer. Weil was an atheist from a secular family – one that even produced frames for images of Catholic saints. But according to the Kolářs, Weil came to consider himself a Jew, because he could not escape anti-Semitism, and in his years of exclusion from the Writers Union, he genuinely embraced his heritage.

When Weil was allowed to publish again, his work was steeped in Jewish history, including his 1958 novel *Harfeník* (The Harpist) and his last novel, the posthumous *Mendelssohn is on the Roof* (1960), which drew from stories passed along orally, such as those that appear in *Lamentation*.

Lamentation for 77,297 Victims goes further than Weil's other works: it recalls the entire history of anti-Semitism from the destruction of Jerusalem in the Jewish bible, through the Nazi era, and into the present day. By linking anecdotes to names, Weil's text returns recognizable human features to those whom oppressors had reduced to numbers. It testifies to the return of Jews to the Czech lands, definitively asserting that those killed and those who survived are Czechs as well as Jews – and as human as they are Czech.

Jiří Kolář's last words to me were "write something nice about Jirka." I hope by bringing this work to readers of English, I am doing it justice. It has been a challenge and an honour to attempt it.

I would like to acknowledge the following individuals for their advice and reactions to this text in chronological order: Veronika Ambros, Nancy Lightfoot, Mirna Solić, Jindřich Toman, Shaughnessey Bishop-Stahl, Erika Esau, my dear friends from writing workshops, and most of all, Barry Burciul.

David Lightfoot defended his Ph.D. thesis on Jiří Weil, the first such work in English, in 2002 at the University of Toronto, where he studied Russian, Czech and Polish literatures. He currently works in Library Services and Knowledge Synthesis at Unity Health Toronto. He is also active in the Toronto Writers Collective.

MODERN CZECH CLASSICS

The modern history of Central Europe is notable for its political and cultural discontinuities and often violent changes, as well as its attempts to preserve and (re)invent traditional cultural identities. This series cultivates contemporary translations of influential literary works that have been unavailable to a global readership due to censorship, the effects of the Cold War, and the frequent political disruptions in Czech publishing and its international ties. Readers of English, in today's cosmopolitan Prague and anywhere in the physical and electronic world, can now become acquainted with works that capture the Central European historical experience – works that have helped express and form Czech and Central European identity, humour, and imagination. Believing that any literary canon can be defined only in dialogue with other cultures, the series publishes classics, often used in Western university courses, as well as (re)discoveries aiming to provide new perspectives in the study of literature, history, and culture. All titles are accompanied by an afterword. Translations are reviewed and circulated in the global scholarly community before publication – this is reflected by our nominations for literary awards.

Published titles

Zdeněk Jirotka: *Saturnin* (2003, 2005, 2009, 2013; pb 2016)
Vladislav Vančura: *Summer of Caprice* (2006; pb 2016)
Karel Poláček: *We Were a Handful* (2007; pb 2016)
Bohumil Hrabal: *Pirouettes on a Postage Stamp* (2008)
Karel Michal: *Everyday Spooks* (2008)
Eduard Bass: *The Chattertooth Eleven* (2009)
Jaroslav Hašek: *Behind the Lines: Bugulma and Other Stories* (2012; pb 2016)
Bohumil Hrabal: *Rambling On* (2014; pb 2016)
Ladislav Fuks: *Of Mice and Mooshaber* (2014)
Josef Jedlička: *Midway upon the Journey of Our Life* (2016)
Jaroslav Durych: *God's Rainbow* (2016)
Ladislav Fuks: *The Cremator* (2016)
Bohuslav Reynek: *The Well at Morning* (2017)
Viktor Dyk: *The Pied Piper* (2017)
Jiří R. Pick: *Society for the Prevention of Cruelty to Animals* (2018)
Views from the Inside: Czech Underground Literature and Culture (1948–1989), ed. M. Machovec (2018)
Ladislav Grosman: *The Shop on Main Street* (2019)
Bohumil Hrabal: *Why I Write? The Early Prose from 1945 to 1952* (2019)
Jiří Pelán: *Bohumil Hrabal: A Full-length Portrait* (2019)
Martin Machovec: *Writing Underground* (2019)
Ludvík Vaculík: *A Czech Dreambook* (2019)
Jaroslav Kvapil: *Rusalka* (2020)

Forthcoming

Jan Procházka: *The Ear*
Ivan M. Jirous: *End of the World. Poetry and Prose*
Jan Čep: *Common Rue*
Jiří Weil: *Moscow – Border*
Jan Zábrana: *All My Life: Pages from a Diary*
Libuše Moníková: *Verklärte Nacht*
Vladislav Vančura: *Fields Arable and of War*